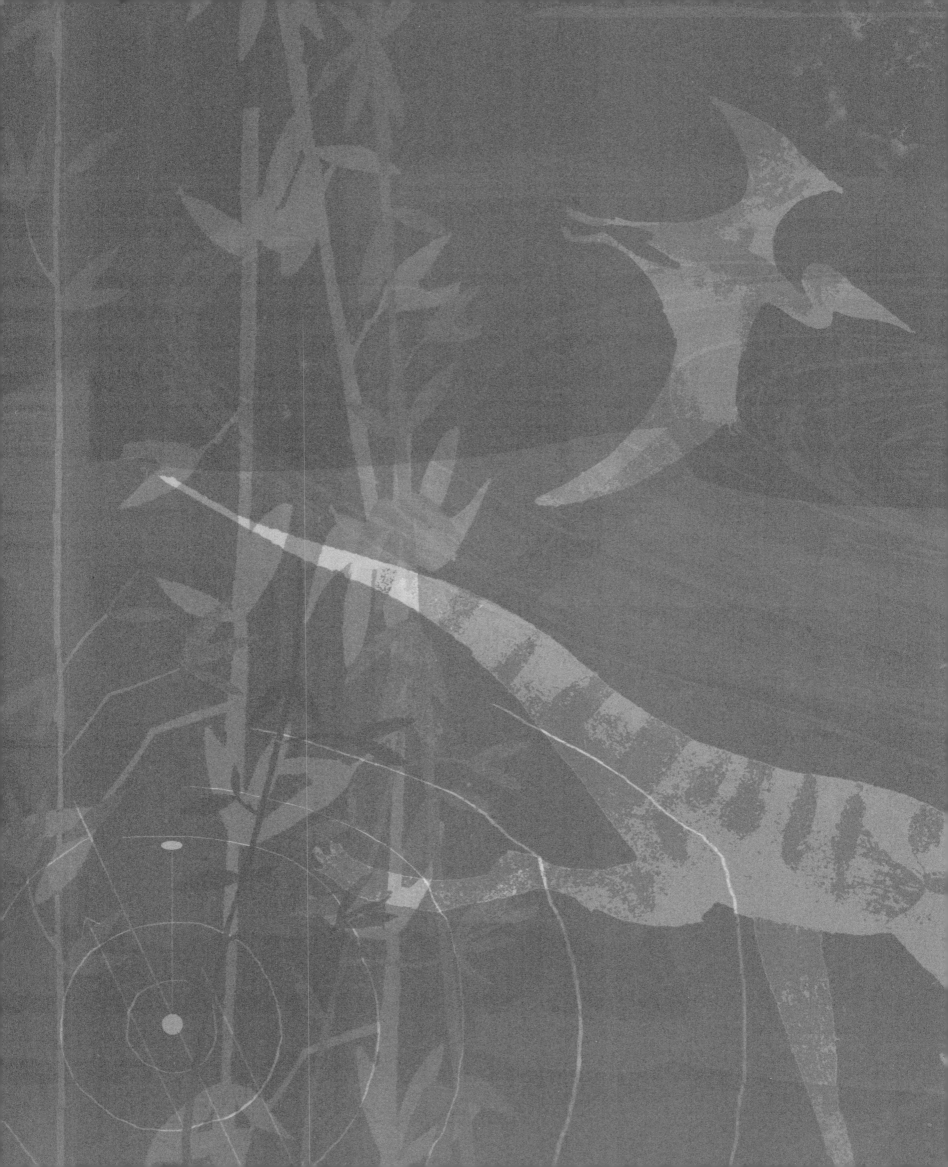

The
EARTH
Book

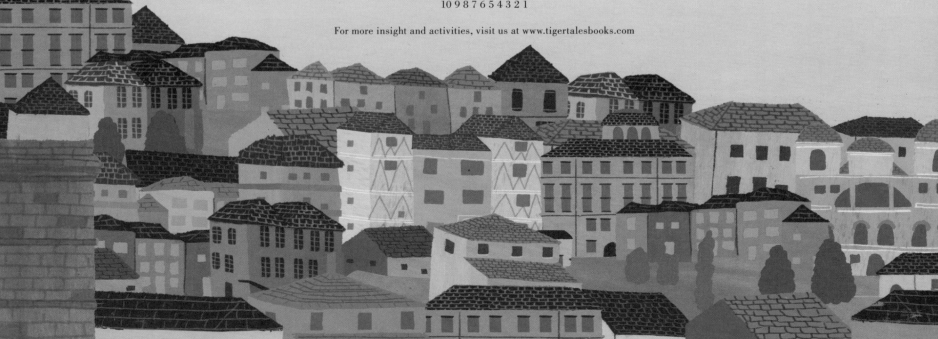

For Lara, Leon, and Sophie,
you mean the world to me.
~J.L.

For Sally.
~T.H.

A WORLD OF CHANGE?
The world is an ever-changing place, as you will discover. Our understanding of it is evolving, too.
New discoveries are there to be made, and new records may replace old ones,
and we will be happy to revise and update information in future editions.

360 DEGREES, an imprint of Tiger Tales
5 River Road, Suite 128, Wilton, CT 06897
Published in the United States 2017
Originally published in Great Britain 2017
by Caterpillar Books
Text by Jonathan Litton
Text copyright © 2017 Caterpillar Books
Illustrated by Thomas Hegbrook
Illustrations copyright © 2017 Caterpillar Books
ISBN-13: 978-1-944530-06-8
ISBN-10: 1-944530-06-1
Printed in China
CPB/1800/0583/0916

For more insight and activities, visit us at www.tigertalesbooks.com

The EARTH Book

BY JONATHAN LITTON

Illustrated by
THOMAS HEGBROOK

Welcome

In the vastness of space lies a tiny sphere that orbits an ordinary, middle-aged star in a quiet backwater of the Milky Way. It's one of billions of trillions of worlds, yet it is the only place we know of that supports life. It's an ever-changing environment, filled with fleeting beauty—99% of species that have ever existed are now extinct for one reason or another. But what remains is a truly astonishing spectacle— a carnival of natural wonders, from lemurs to lemmings and giant sequoias to Antarctic mosses. In recent times, Earth's story has become intertwined with the human story, as we have created new urban and rural habitats and have harnessed energy and resources to meet our needs. To better understand and nurture our fragile little home, let's go on a voyage of discovery to the four corners of the globe....

EARTH
at a glance

There's so much to explore, so where to start? At the beginning, of course! First we investigate Earth's origins, its composition, and its dynamic processes. Then we move on to the fascinating array of life, from the earliest beings to emerge from the primordial soup to a cacophony of present-day wonders from a variety of families and habitats. Next it's a globetrotting tour of ecosystems and environments, encompassing both the expected and the unusual...such as penguins in a rainforest! Our final chapter is a look at the human world, and considers questions such as where people came from, how we divided the planet into countries and continents, and who are some of the most influential Earthlings in our history. We hope you enjoy this grand pictorial tour of our humble home.

Physical Earth

Explore the inner workings of the Earth, from earthquakes and volcanoes to thunderstorms and tsunamis.

Life on Earth

Learn about many of the billions of Earth's inhabitants, from the miniature to the mighty, and from the past to the present.

Earth Regions

Investigate a rich variety of ecosystems from all corners of the globe, including deserts, rainforests, oceans, and islands.

Human Planet

Ponder the human impact on the planet, from migration and population growth to cities and sustainability.

Physical EARTH

*"Look again at that dot.
That's here. That's home. That's us."*

~ Carl Sagan

Our planet is insignificant in the vastness of space, but hugely significant for the plants and animals that call it home. It's a middle-aged space rock, about halfway through its natural life, containing multiple layers of intrigue, from its super-heated core to its outermost atmosphere. It's the only planet we know of that experiences plate tectonics, and it's also unique in supporting a water-based weather system. Sometimes we surface-dwellers get a hint of the planet's raw power through earthquakes, volcanoes, tornadoes, and tsunamis. At other times we can sit back and marvel at Earth's natural beauty.

How the Earth *was* FORMED

For about 9 billion years, the universe was Earthless. Then, about 4.6 billion years ago, a giant dust cloud (made of dust from exploded stars) experienced a remarkable transformation. Matter was sucked into a solid center because of gravity, and a hot, dense star was born: the Sun.

Although most of the dust cloud formed the Sun, a tiny amount was left swirling around the center, in what is called a protoplanetary disc. About 100 million years after the formation of the Sun, gravity molded that disc into the planets, moons, and comets of the solar system, including Earth.

So there you have it: Earth is made from ancient stardust, as are all Earthlings.

THE EARTH'S TWIN
Many scientists believe that Earth once had a twin planet named Theia. One day, their paths crossed and there was a huge collision. Earth absorbed most of Theia, but some material was ejected, which formed the Moon. This is sometimes called the Big Splat Theory.

LAW OF ATTRACTION
Gravity acts to pull things together. The heavier something is, the stronger the force of attraction, so the Sun has a huge gravitational pull.

Stages of creation

Our knowledge of the formation of the solar system is evolving, but most scientists have settled upon a standard theory.

SUPERNOVA EXPLOSION

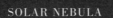

SOLAR NEBULA

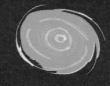

PROTOPLANETARY DISC

CENTER OF ATTENTION
The Sun contains 99.86%
of the matter in the solar
system, condensed into a
super-heated sphere.

SPACE ROCKS
Most of the remaining rocky
matter formed planets and
moons, but some became
"dwarf planets" and asteroids.

We believe that our solar system underwent the beautiful and spectacular sequence of events below, spread across hundreds of millions of years.

GRAVITATIONAL SCULPTING OF THE SOLAR SYSTEM   PLANET FORMATION AND STABILIZATION OF SYSTEM

VIRGO III GROUPS

NGC 7582

VIRGO CLUSTER

LOCAL GROUP
SCULPTOR

MAFFEI

FORNAX CLUSTER

URSA MAJOR
GROUPS

ERIDANUS CLUSTER

YOU ARE HERE

OBSERVABLE UNIVERSE
The observable universe is about 92 billion light years across. At this scale, our galaxy is much too small to see.

LOCAL SUPERCLUSTERS
Within our local superclusters of galaxies, we can just about spot our galaxy: the Milky Way.

MILKY WAY
Within the Milky Way, the solar system is but a tiny dot on one of the spiral arms. We are out in the suburbs of our interstellar "city"!

THIRD ROCK *from the* SUN

Space is huge and Earth is tiny. You have to zoom in a very long way with our cosmic microscope to pick out our planet among the vastness of space. Locating our home within the universe can be a humbling experience. Given how small, fragile, and tiny our home is, we need to cherish and look after it—after all, it's the only place we know about on which we could hope to survive.

THIRD ROCK FROM THE SUN
Earth makes up only 0.000003% of the solar system's mass, compared to a whopping 99.86% for the Sun. But small is good for us—we are just the right size to support an atmosphere. We are also in the "Goldilocks zone" in terms of distance from the Sun—too close and we'd overheat, and too far away and we'd be too cold.

NEIGHBORING WORLDS
Within the solar system there are eight main planets, plus a number of dwarf planets, comets, and asteroids. Jupiter is by far the largest—it is more than twice as heavy as all the others combined.

MERCURY

VENUS

EARTH

MARS

CERES
(dwarf planet)

JUPITER

SATURN

URANUS

YOU ARE HERE

PALE BLUE DOT
This famous image was photographed by Voyager 1 as it exited the solar system. Earth took up less than one pixel!

OTHER EARTHS?
One of the most Earth-like worlds observed is named Kepler-452b, but we have no indication it supports life.

DISTANT WORLDS
Pluto was downgraded from planet to dwarf planet in 2006. Since then, even more distant dwarf planets have been observed, including Eris (shown), Sedna, Makemake, and V774014.

NEPTUNE

PLUTO (& CHARON)
(dwarf planet)

ERIS
(dwarf planet)

Where does EARTH end and SPACE begin?

Officially, space begins 62 miles (100 km) up, but that's a very artificial line to draw! Real lines are observed in the form of layers —the atmosphere is made up of several sections with distinct characteristics.

EXOSPHERE
This really is the limit of the atmosphere—molecules are attracted to the Earth by gravity, but are spaced very far apart, meaning they don't behave like a gas. The exosphere thins out to deep, dark space.

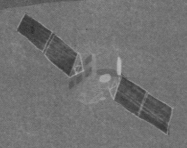

THERMOSPHERE
Temperatures in the thermosphere can reach higher than 3,600°F (2,000°C), but because the gases are so spread out, it wouldn't feel that hot if you were to reach out and touch it! The International Space Station orbits in this layer.

MESOSPHERE
A handful of balloons have made it to the mesosphere, but this layer remains one of the least understood of our atmosphere.

STRATOSPHERE
The top of Mount Everest sits in the stratosphere, and some birds and bacteria can survive at this height.

TROPOSPHERE
The vast majority of the atmosphere is in the lowest layer, called the troposphere. It contains all of our weather and clouds.

EARTHQUAKES and VOLCANOES

Usually we stand on solid ground, but every now and then, here and there, the interior of the Earth creates a much less stable environment. Earthquakes and volcanoes both give us glimpses of the inner workings of the planet and show how ours is a dynamic, ever-changing world.

Earthquakes

The Earth's crust is divided into tectonic plates, which very gradually move toward each other or apart from each other. The places where plates meet are called fault lines and are home to tremendous forces that can build up for decades or centuries. Eventually, something gives way and the plates will suddenly slip against each other —this is an earthquake. The underground center of the earthquake is called the focus, and the nearest point to this on the surface is known as the epicenter.

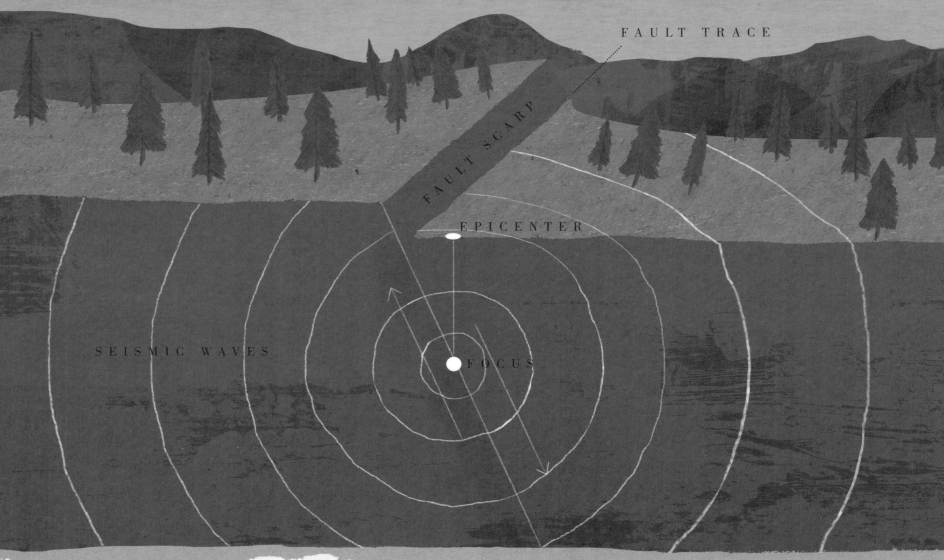

FAULT TRACE

FAULT SCARP

EPICENTER

SEISMIC WAVES

FOCUS

EURASIAN PLATE

NORTH AMERICAN PLATE

RING OF FIRE

CARIBBEAN PLATE

PACIFIC PLATE

NAZCA PLATE

SOUTH AMERICAN PLATE

AUSTRALIAN PLATE

ANTARCTIC PLATE

SCOTIA PLATE

ANTARCTIC PLATE

EURASIAN PLATE

AFRICAN PLATE

ARABIC PLATE

INDIAN PLATE

Ring of Fire

Here you can see the major tectonic plates of the Earth. The boundaries of the Pacific Plate are a hotspot for earthquakes and volcanoes, and it has become known as the Ring of Fire (but it is actually in the shape of a horseshoe). 90% of earthquakes and 75% of the world's volcanoes are located here, making it a beautiful but dangerous place. Countries like Japan, Chile, and Indonesia are used to regular disasters, and everyone from office workers to schoolchildren will practice disaster relief drills on a regular basis.

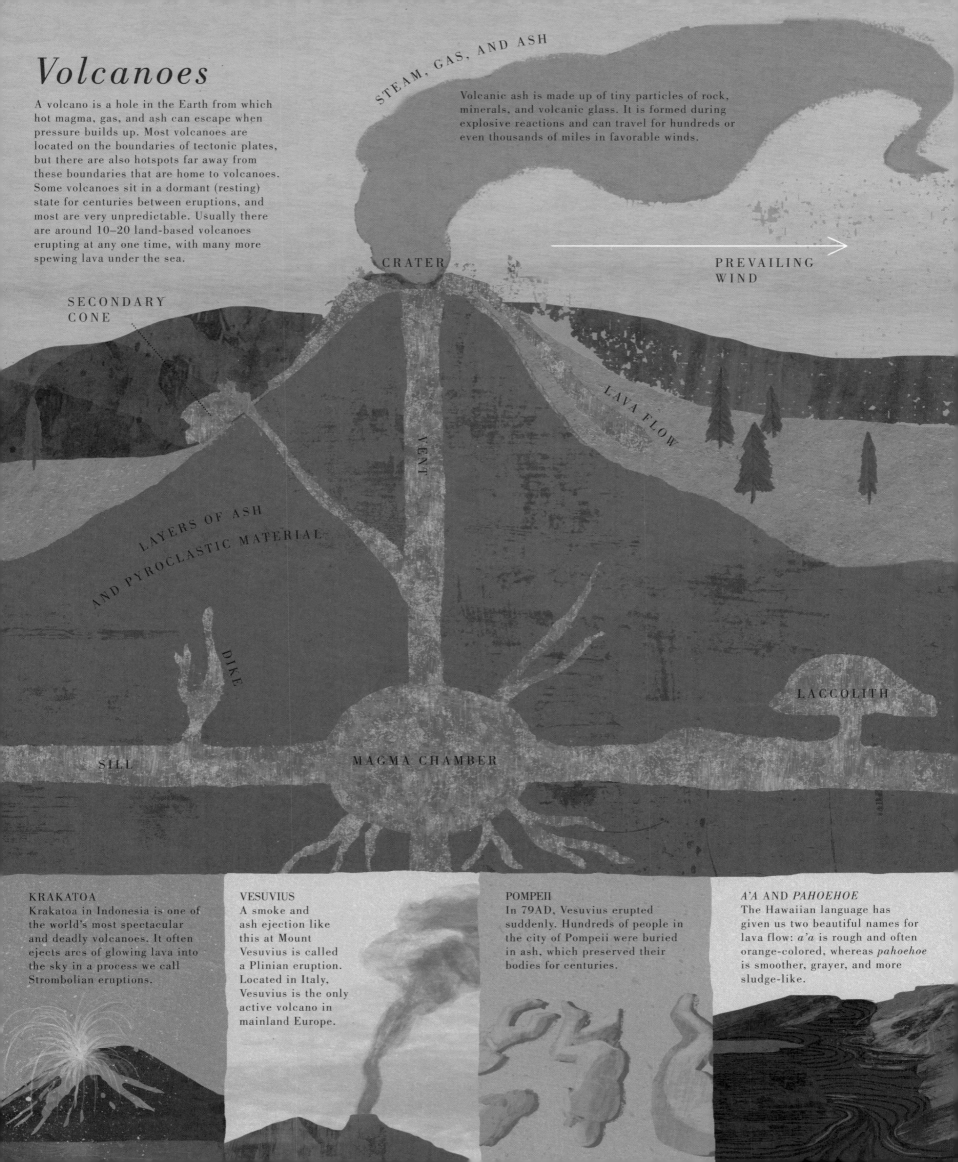

Volcanoes

A volcano is a hole in the Earth from which hot magma, gas, and ash can escape when pressure builds up. Most volcanoes are located on the boundaries of tectonic plates, but there are also hotspots far away from these boundaries that are home to volcanoes. Some volcanoes sit in a dormant (resting) state for centuries between eruptions, and most are very unpredictable. Usually there are around 10–20 land-based volcanoes erupting at any one time, with many more spewing lava under the sea.

STEAM, GAS, AND ASH

Volcanic ash is made up of tiny particles of rock, minerals, and volcanic glass. It is formed during explosive reactions and can travel for hundreds or even thousands of miles in favorable winds.

CRATER

PREVAILING WIND

SECONDARY CONE

LAVA FLOW

VENT

LAYERS OF ASH AND PYROCLASTIC MATERIAL

DIKE

LACCOLITH

SILL

MAGMA CHAMBER

KRAKATOA
Krakatoa in Indonesia is one of the world's most spectacular and deadly volcanoes. It often ejects arcs of glowing lava into the sky in a process we call Strombolian eruptions.

VESUVIUS
A smoke and ash ejection like this at Mount Vesuvius is called a Plinian eruption. Located in Italy, Vesuvius is the only active volcano in mainland Europe.

POMPEII
In 79AD, Vesuvius erupted suddenly. Hundreds of people in the city of Pompeii were buried in ash, which preserved their bodies for centuries.

A'A AND *PAHOEHOE*
The Hawaiian language has given us two beautiful names for lava flow: *a'a* is rough and often orange-colored, whereas *pahoehoe* is smoother, grayer, and more sludge-like.

The Water Cycle

Understanding the passage of water from ground to air and back again is a key ingredient for any budding meteorologist (weather expert). See if you can follow the path of water, from evaporation and transpiration to precipitation, then streamflow or infiltration, and back to the beginning again.

Clouds

Clouds form when water vapor condenses into tiny water droplets or ice crystals and settle on dust particles in the atmosphere. They come in many shapes and sizes, and not all lead to rain and snow.

PRECIPITATION
(rain, snow, sleet, or hail)

CIRRUS

Delicate, and formed of ice crystals.

ALTOCUMULUS

Forms in sheets.

ALTOSTRATUS

Gray or bluish.

SNOWMELT

RUNOFF

SNOW
Snow occurs when temperatures are low and ice crystals in clouds stick together forming snowflakes. Because these snowflakes are heavy, they fall to the ground.

Runoff is the flow of water from land into streams, rivers, lakes, and oceans.

STREAMFLOW

SEASONS
The tilt of the Earth means one end is closer to the Sun than the other. This is the cause of the season — when it is summer in the north it is winter in the south, and vice versa.

RIVERS AND LAKES
Freshwater lakes contain about seven-eighths of the world's fresh *surface* water. Rivers contain a much smaller amount.

TRANSPIRATION
(evaporation from plant leaves)

SPRING
Sometimes groundwater resurfaces through holes in the ground called springs.

INFILTRATION
(water seeps into ground)

GROUNDWATER
Large volumes of water are stored beneath the ground in spaces between rocks. Most of our drinking water is sourced from natural underwater reservoirs called aquifers.

FLOW

TAKE-UP BY PLANTS AND TREES

STORAGE

CIRROSTRATUS

A very high and thin cloud.

SUNSHINE
The Sun warms the atmosphere, land, and oceans, and is the main driving force behind our weather. No sun; no weather!

CUMULONIMBUS

RAINBOW
Sunlight reflected and bent by water droplets in the atmosphere creates one of nature's most beautiful displays.

The super-tall thunderstorm cloud.

CUMULUS

Said to resemble cauliflower.

TRANSPIRATION
(evaporation from plant leaves)

How the
WEATHER
WORKS

Weather is one of the most frequent topics of conversation and affects people's activities around the world. While we understand the main principles that drive different types of weather, scientists believe that weather is so sensitive that we will never be able to collect enough data to predict it with 100% accuracy... so have umbrellas handy!

THUNDER AND LIGHTNING
Thunderstorm clouds can be taller than 6.2 miles (10 km) from base to top. Lightning is caused by electricity flowing between negatively charged clouds and positively charged objects on the ground, and thunder is the explosive sound produced by the lightning.

RUNOFF

WIND
The wind usually blows in a certain direction, depending on where you are on the planet. This is because the atmosphere is divided into cells of circulating air, which rise and sink in a familiar pattern.

Sinking air
Rising air

LAND

EVAPORATION

WEATHER PREDICTION
Instruments on the ground and in the air give meteorologists thousands of data points, from which they predict the future. It's not a perfect science, though— sometimes they are wrong!

WEATHER AND CLIMATE
Weather refers to short-term phenomena such as rain, snow, and wind, whereas climate refers to long-term patterns of weather.

OCEAN
The oceans contain about 97% of the world's water.

WEATHER MODIFICATION
Since ancient times, people have attempted to control the weather, and modern science makes this a reality. Rainfall can be encouraged using cloud-seeding planes that inject silver iodide into clouds, maximizing the chances of ice crystals forming.

WEIRD WEATHER
There have been occasional reports of "non-aqueous rain," meaning things other than water dropping from the sky...things such as fish, toads, worms, and spiders! These rare events are thought to be caused by tornado-like winds.

HEART OF THE PLANET
Recent research has found that the inner core is itself made of two
distinct layers: the outer inner core, and the inner inner core!

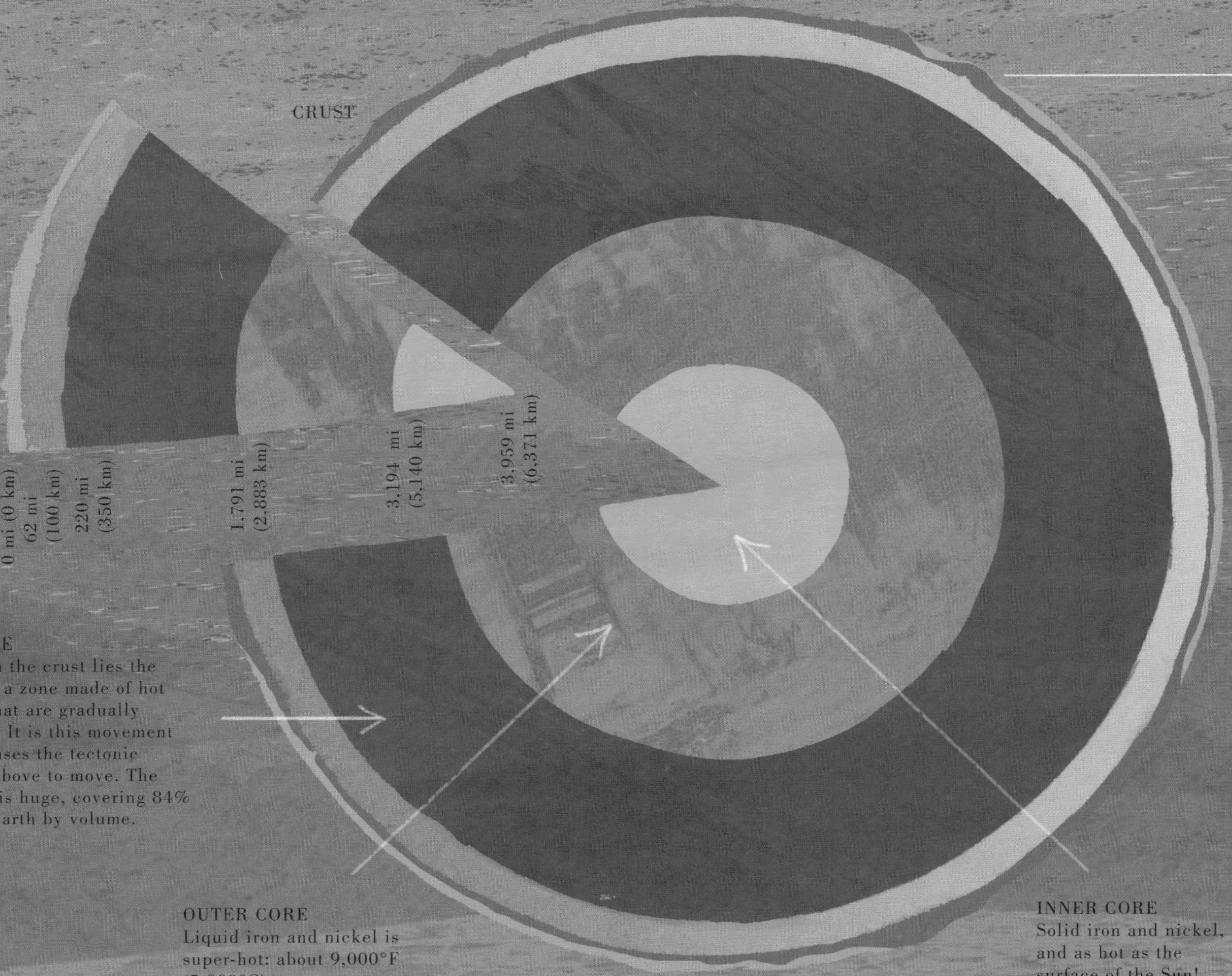

CRUST

0 mi (0 km)
62 mi (100 km)
220 mi (350 km)
1,791 mi (2,883 km)
3,194 mi (5,140 km)
3,959 mi (6,371 km)

MANTLE
Beneath the crust lies the
mantle, a zone made of hot
rocks that are gradually
moving. It is this movement
that causes the tectonic
plates above to move. The
mantle is huge, covering 84%
of the Earth by volume.

OUTER CORE
Liquid iron and nickel is
super-hot: about 9,000°F
(5,000°C) on average.

INNER CORE
Solid iron and nickel,
and as hot as the
surface of the Sun!

Journey to the
CENTER *of the* EARTH

The center of the Earth is as hot as the surface of the Sun, so we couldn't ever go on a real
journey there. Drilling more than a few miles into the crust becomes impossible because
of the scorching temperatures, so most of our information about the Earth's interior comes
from indirect observations, such as how seismic waves travel, and what chemical forms
can exist at certain densities. Very recently, we've discovered an "inner inner core"—
an extra layer to our planetary onion!

The Earth is smoother than a bowling ball—the highest mountains create bumps of less than 0.1% of the Earth's radius.

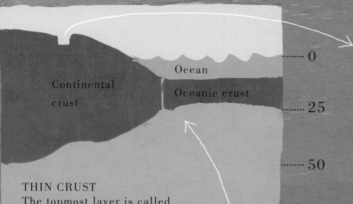

Ocean

Continental crust

Oceanic crust

.... 0

.... 25

.... 50

....

.... 100

....

.... 150

....

.... 200

THIN CRUST
The topmost layer is called the crust, and consists of rocks of various types—both on land and under the oceans. Continental crust is usually 19–31 miles (30–50 km) thick, whereas oceanic crust is about 3–6 miles (5–10 km) thick.

THE MOHO
The area between the crust and mantle (the second layer) is known as the Moho, which is named after a Croatian seismologist (earthquake expert) by the name of Andrija Mohorovicic.

SCRATCHING THE SURFACE
Humans have barely scratched the surface of our planet. The deepest we've dug is 7.6 miles (12.3 km) into the continental crust at a remote site in Russia. Known as the Kola Superdeep Borehole, this hole set the world depth record in 1979, and drilling underneath the white tower continued until 1992. However, the team experienced higher temperatures than expected, and the project was abandoned.

Now the tower is gone, and only a rusty metal cap stops anyone from peering down the deepest hole in the world!

Buried Treasure
The Earth's crust mostly consists of oxygen and silicon, but there are also much more valuable substances hiding underground. These include...

GOLD
Although gold has been mined for more than 1,000 years, if we put all the gold together into a single cube, each side would measure only 69 feet (21 m). It's a pretty rare metal!

CARBON: DIAMOND
Diamond is one of the most attractive substances on (and in) Earth. It's simply carbon atoms arranged in a crystal structure.

PLUTONIUM
This gray element is very rare and very radioactive, meaning it emits rays harmful to humans. However, if handled safely, its power can be used to generate electricity.

PLATINUM
Rarer than both silver and gold, this expensive metal is used in jewelry, cars, and electronics.

CARBON: GRAPHITE
The same element that makes diamonds also forms graphite, which we use in pencils.

SILVER
Sometimes considered to be gold's ugly sister, almost 10 times as much silver has been mined as gold.

TORNADO

In the right conditions, a thunderstorm can produce a swirling column of air called a tornado. Winds can reach 190 miles per hour (300 kph), and the forward motion can be up to 19 miles per hour (13 kph). Tornadoes can lift cars and even houses clean off the ground — it's best not to get too close, but some storm chasers make this their hobby!

LIGHTNING

Five times as hot as the surface of the Sun, yet only 1 inch (2.5 cm) wide, lightning occurs when a negatively charged thundercloud travels across positively charged ground — the lightning is the flow of electricity that completes this spectacular circuit.

POWERFUL
Planet

Nature can unleash some powerful events — spectacular to see from a distance, but dangerous and sometimes deadly to experience up close. From volcanoes and earthquakes to hurricanes and tornadoes, it's wise to be clued in to our planet's raw power.

TSUNAMI

Undersea earthquakes cause huge waves, which can reach 100 feet (30 m) in height when they hit the coast. The impact of tsunamis can be devastating — about a quarter of a million people died following the 2004 Indian Ocean tsunami.

FLOOD

A flood is an overflow of water on land that is usually dry. They are becoming much more common due to human activity such as covering ground in concrete, preventing water from draining naturally through the soil. Deforestation also leads to more frequent flooding.

HURRICANE

A hurricane can stretch almost 620 miles (1,000 km) across and can have spiraling wind speeds of more than 190 miles per hour (300 kph). These huge oceanic storms gain heat and energy from the warm ocean waters and cause widespread destruction if they pass over land.

— The eye of the storm

VOLCANO

Volcanoes are tremendously powerful. The biggest blasts can be heard over tens or even hundreds of miles, and ejected material can travel over thousands of miles. Scientists in Iceland are trying to harness this raw power for electricity generation.

LANDSLIDE

Ground isn't always as solid as it seems. If the elements such as rocks and soil are not bound strongly together, tons of earth can slide due to gravity, particularly down slopes or cliffs. Water loosening rocks is often a trigger for such situations.

AVALANCHE

An avalanche is similar to a landslide, but instead of land that is sliding, it's snow! As snow is not bound together like rocks, more and more snow will become involved in the downward motion, creating a potentially deadly situation for anyone below.

EARTHQUAKE

Providing a front-row seat to the raw power of planet Earth, earthquakes are clearly tremendously powerful. They are commonly measured on the Richter Scale, which describes the energy, and the Mercalli Scale, which represents the impact on humans. A "Big One" is predicted to occur every 10–50 years, causing devastation to the affected area.

SINKHOLE

Sometimes the surface of the Earth collapses, and huge holes appear that can swallow cars, houses, and even buildings. Although the holes seem to form in an instant, they are usually caused by water creating underground caverns over many months, before the surface finally collapses. Sinkholes are found all over the world, and we have no way of predicting when or where the next might be.

PLATE TECTONICS

The Earth's crust is divided into tectonic plates, which move very gradually—a typical speed is 0.4 inches (1 cm) per year. Over millions of years, such tiny movements have resulted in continents crossing half the globe! In the age of the dinosaurs, the Earth had a super-continent called Pangaea.

225 million years ago

150 million years ago

Present day

Ever-changing EARTH

The Earth has changed dramatically over time. It has been much hotter (in the primordial phase) and much colder (in the Ice Ages), the continents have been in different positions, dinosaurs evolved and became extinct, volcanoes and mountains have sprung up, and former land has been lost to the sea, to give just a few examples. Most of these changes occur very slowly—sometimes over hundreds of millions of years—but occasionally big changes can occur in the blink of an eye.

COASTAL EROSION

As waves lap against a coastline, little by little they loosen the soil and rocks, and take bits of the land away forever. Sometimes this can happen very dramatically—in parts of the north of England, the coastline is retreating at around 6.6 feet (2 m) per year, taking entire houses with it during storms!

GLACIERS

Ice is even more powerful than liquid water at shaping the land. Glaciers act like slow-moving solid rivers, and the ice molds the land it slides over, carving out smooth hills and valleys. Global warming means many glaciers are in danger of melting at the moment.

GEYSERS

In the right conditions, steam and water underground will erupt from small vents or holes called geysers. These "water and steam volcanoes" are extremely rare and show the power inside the Earth—the water is usually heated 1.2 miles (2 km) beneath the surface before bursting out in spectacular fashion.

MOUNTAIN FORMATION

When continental plates collide, the top part of the Earth's crust can be forced upward, forming mountain ranges. Mount Everest is growing by about 0.16 inches (4 mm) a year as the Indian Plate and Eurasian Plate continue to crash into each other, as they have done for 50 million years.

PINGOS

Ice is a fantastic sculptor of land, and nowhere is that more evident than in the hills of the far north. Called pingos (what a wonderful name!), these smooth-sided mounds form only in Arctic conditions where ice freezes and thaws each year. Northern Canada is a hotspot for these cold-spots.

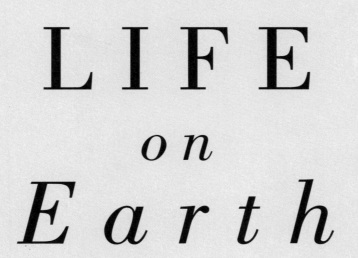

LIFE
on
Earth

"The good man is the friend of all living things."

~ Mahatma Gandhi

Our planet has proved to be the perfect incubator for life. Since single-celled organisms first emerged from the primordial soup about 3.8 billion years ago, there have been around 1 billion species—10 million of which are living today. The diversity and ingenuity of life is incredible, from plants that withstand Antarctic winters to hardy tardigrades that can survive in space. Plants, fungi, bacteria, archea, and other life forms are explored in these pages, as well as all creatures great and small, and we journey back into prehistory in addition to looking at Earth's current cast of inhabitants.

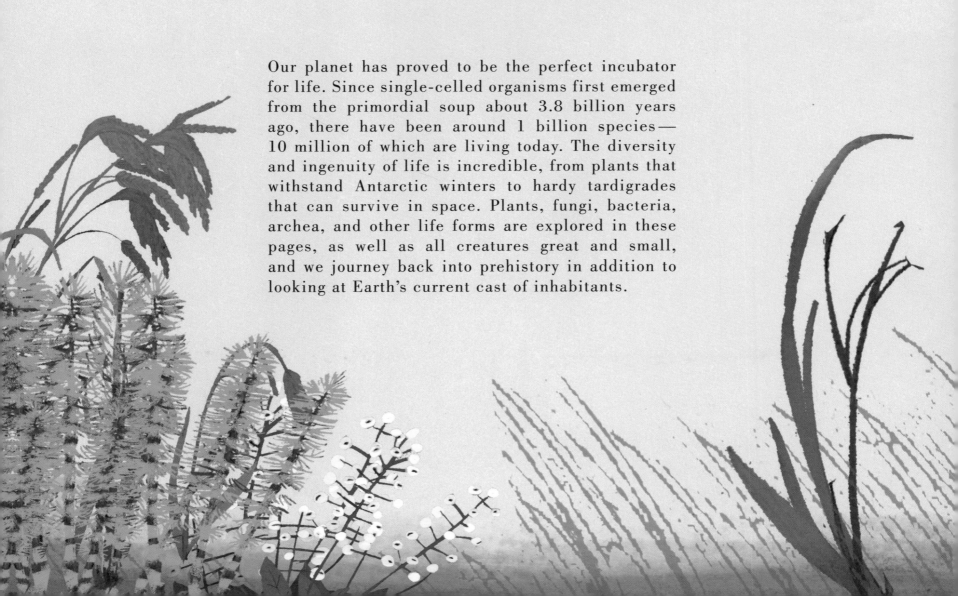

LUCA: THE SEED OF LIFE
All present life is thought to have evolved from a single-celled
organism called LUCA (Last Universal Common Ancestor),
which lived about 3.6 billion years ago.

Eudicots
Monocots
Gnetophytes
Conifers
Magnoliids
Ginkgo
Star anise
Ferns
Cycads
Horsetails
Water lilies
Whisk ferns
Amborellales
Club mosses & relatives
Hornworts
PLANTAE
Mosses
Green algae
Liverworts
ARCHAEOPLASTIDS
Glaucophytes
Apicomplexans
Red algae
dinoflagellates
Foraminiferans
ciliates
RHIZARIA
ALVEOLATES
Actinopods
Water molds
STRAMENOPILES
CHROMALVEOLATES
Brown algae
Diatoms
Cryptomonads
Golden algae
Haptophytes
Spirochetes
Green sulfur
Cyanobacteria
EXCAVATES
Flavobacteria
Gram-positive
Proteobacteria
Planctomyces
Chlamydiae
Radioresistant micrococci & relatives
BACTERIA
Green non-sulfur bacteria & relatives
Thermotogae

Glomeromycota
Sac fungi
Club fungi
Blastocladiomycota
Neocallimastigomycota
Chytrids
Microsporidia

FUNGI
ANIMALIA
CHOANOFLAGELLATE
AMOEBOZOA
ARCHAEA

A LIVING TREE OF LIFE
Our understanding of life is evolving. Microscopic organisms in particular are poorly understood,
and scientists are discovering more about the relationships between the lower branches of
the tree. So this tree of life should be seen as a living thing itself, with new shoots capable of
sprouting and older branches dying out.

Millipedes & relatives

Crustaceans

Spiders & relatives

Insects & relatives

Velvet worms

Tardigrades

Bryozoans

Flat worms

Rotifers

Ribbon worms

Birds

Crocodilians

Lizards & relatives

Turtles

Mammals

Roundworms

Lamp shells

Amphibians

Segmented worms

Lungfishes

Mollusks

Lobe-finned fishes

Ray-finned fishes

Arrow worms

Chondrichthyans

Lampreys

Sea stars & relatives

Lancelets

Sea squirts

Hag fishes

Sea jellies & relatives

Sponges

Comb jellies

Slime molds

Amoeba and relatives

Crenarchaeota

Euryarchaeota

Korarchaeota

Nanoarchaeota

Thaumarchaeota

TREE *of* LIFE

Our best estimate is that about 1 billion species have existed on Earth, of which 99% are now extinct. However, the remaining 1% is amazingly rich in diversity, from bacteria to blue whales and from mushrooms to Christmas trees. All life is related, and all began from one original single-celled species in the primordial phase of the planet. We can divide life via branches on a tree—the big branches represent kingdoms such as plants, animals, and bacteria, and the smaller branches represent subdivisions. Even the twigs and leaves at the ends can represent mind-bogglingly large numbers of species—there are around 5,400 mammal species and 1 million insect species—but we can only show one example from each.

POLAR ICE
(ARCTIC &
ANTARCTIC)

TUNDRA
(POLAR &
ALPINE)

TAIGA
(BOREAL
FOREST)

TEMPERATE
DECIDUOUS
FOREST

TROPICAL
FOREST
(RAINFOREST)

SAVANNA
(TROPICAL
GRASSLAND)

CHAPARRAL
(HOT, DRY
HEATHLAND)

TEMPERATE
GRASSLAND

DESERT
(SUBTROPICAL)

Polar bear

American bison

American alligator

Hummingbird

Eurasian red squirrel

CHAPARRAL
Small corners of six continents are home to this habitat, which is characterized by dry weather and short, woody-rooted, scrub-like plants. It is somewhat similar to the desert environment, with animals such as lizards, coyotes, and jack rabbits needing fewer adaptations.

Arabian camel

Mountain gorilla

TROPICAL RAINFOREST
These are the most biodiverse of all the land regions and are teeming with animal life of all shapes and sizes. Piranhas, parakeets, hummingbirds, jaguars, tree frogs, and lemurs make their homes here, to name but a few examples of the many millions of rainforest species.

TEMPERATE GRASSLAND
Grasses are the dominant plant species here, and the region is also known as the plains in North America and the pampas in South America. As grasses are quite nutrient-poor, animals tend to need large areas to roam in order to sustain themselves. Because of this, biodiversity is relatively low, but well-adapted animals can exhibit huge populations, like the bison whose herds could be 1 million strong before human intervention.

Piranha

Three-toed sloth

Parrot

SAVANNA
Typically located between rainforest and desert regions, these areas are hot and support grasses, shrubs, and isolated trees. Plentiful grasses support large herbivores, and the scarcity of water means that many species gather together around waterholes. The African savanna is where you will find species such as elephants, zebras, and giraffes rubbing shoulders, with lions not too far from sight!

Animal HABITATS

We categorize the world into ecoregions or biomes that support different types of life. You can see from the map that there are patterns to these regions, and that there are gradual trends— interrupted by oceans, mountains, and anomolies —from cold environments at the poles to tropical environments near the equator. Climate and geology help determine the plant life that grows in each area, which in turn determines the animal life that can be supported—both the types of creatures and the sizes of their populations.

POLAR ICE
There is no plant life in regions permanently covered with ice, so life from the surrounding oceans usually supports the food web. Because of the harsh conditions, there are no permanent animal inhabitants on the ice caps larger than 0.12 inches (3 mm)—the polar bears of the north and penguins of the south are just visitors!

Emperor penguin

TUNDRA
These treeless plains are cold and frosty, with few nutrients in the soil and very short growing seasons. This limits the plant life, and animals such as reindeer are well adapted to sniff out mosses and lichen between blankets of snow. Animals typically have to cover large areas to find enough food to survive, so biodiversity is low here.

TAIGA
These huge forests consist mainly of coniferous trees and collectively form the world's largest biome. Owing to extremely harsh winters, they support a relatively low number of animals, but those that do make their home here often have large ranges, such as the brown bear and the Siberian tiger.

Reindeer

Wild boar

European otter

Siberian tiger

TEMPERATE DECIDUOUS FOREST
Unlike the evergreen trees of the taiga further north, these forests are characterized by the annual growing and shedding of the leafy canopy. Life is abundant in the spring and summer, when insects eat the growing tree leaves, often to be eaten in turn by birds and mammals, but visitors are far fewer in the autumn and winter.

Fennec fox

Asian elephant

Sumatran orangutan

DESERT
Subtropical deserts are hot during the day and cold at night, and receive very little moisture. Animals have to be well-adapted to cope with this trio of potential difficulties. The camel is one of the largest desert-dwellers, and smaller species include addax, sidewinders, jerboa, beetles, termites, and scorpions—all of which display adaptations for survival in this extreme environment.

Ring-tailed lemur

African elephant

Bird of paradise

Christmas Island crab

Kangaroo

Blue whale

Tasmanian devil

MARINE HABITATS
By far the biggest living area on the planet is underwater. The marine habitat extends from the surface all the way to the seafloor, which can reach 6.8 miles (11 km) deep in the largest ocean trenches. The variety of life is enormous, from microscopic plankton to mighty whales, and the deep-sea environment is so vast and otherworldly that many species are as yet unknown to science.

URBAN ENVIRONMENT
You won't find this marked on many maps of ecoregions, but the Earth is an increasingly urban place, and by some definitions is a biome in its own right. Animals such as rats, pigeons, cockroaches, and squirrels have famously colonized our cities and towns, lured by warmth, shelter, and abundant food sources. Indeed, only one Canadian province has held off the advance of the brown rat —pretty much every other place of major population has been conquered by this large, city-loving rodent.

Brown rat

PLANTS and TREES

1. POTATO PLANT
If you bury a potato in the ground, a potato plant should grow above ground, which will then produce more potatoes underground!

2. MAPLE TREE
Maple trees have existed for 100 million years. They produce a sugary sap called maple syrup, which is enjoyed worldwide.

3. MISTLETOE
This plant is a parasite that grows on the branches of trees or shrubs. It has root-like haustoria, which tap into the water and nutrients from the host tree.

4. RHUBARB
There is a technique for cultivating rhubarb in dark sheds—this "forced rhubarb" shoots up so quickly that you can hear it grow!

5. "DOLL'S EYE" (WHITE BANEBERRY)
The unusual-looking berries on this plant are so poisonous to humans that eating even a single berry could result in death.

6. RICE
Rice requires a lot of water, so is grown by farmers in wet paddy fields. It is one of the world's most important food crops.

7. SUNFLOWER
The sunflower's head turns during the day to receive maximum sunlight. The seeds are arranged in beautiful mathematical patterns.

8. CORN
This domesticated plant belongs to the grass family. It is a vital human food source and is farmed on every continent except Antarctica.

9. SCREWPINE
The above-ground root system helps to protect the screwpine against heavy winds. A taproot helps extract nutrients from salty soils.

10. HORSETAIL
The horsetail has no leaves or flowers, and the modern version is closely related to giant versions that thrived 270 million years ago.

11. BAMBOO
In order to reach sunlight in dense forests, this fast-growing plant can shoot up by an astonishing 3.3 feet (1 m) in a single day!

There are more than 300,000 plant species, ranging from wolffia, which is smaller than a grain of rice, to redwood trees reaching more than 330 feet (100 m) tall. Trees are a subgroup of plants, characterized by having a trunk and branches. They are vital for maintaining oxygen levels in the atmosphere.

12. PINEAPPLE
Pineapples grow on plants rather than trees, and it takes around three years for each fruit to fully ripen.

13. MIRACLE FRUIT
This small fruit is quite remarkable—whatever you eat after it will taste sweet...even a lemon! It is very aptly named!

14. CONIFER
This ancient branch of the tree family dates back 290 million years. The tallest and oldest trees alive today are both conifers.

15. VENUS FLYTRAP
This carnivorous plant attracts insects not for pollination but for food! It ordinarily grows in soils that are poor in nutrients, so it seeks the nourishment it requires from insects, or even small frogs! Each "trap" only lasts for about 5 or 6 catches before it withers and dies, and the plant grows a new one to replace it.

Remarkable Species

Every species is remarkable, but some are more remarkable than others! Prepare to be amazed by the plants and animals on this page, which are all extraordinary in their own way. From huge appetites to super-sized flowers, many have made incredible adaptations to help them live in their environments.

THORNY DEVIL
The body shape of this desert lizard helps it collect water, which it can lap up with its tongue. However, studies show that it can also *drink through its skin!*

LONDON UNDERGROUND MOSQUITO
Although the majority of the species lives in the London Underground (as you'd expect from the name), specimens have also been found in other man-made underground systems around the world.

OLD TJIKKO
This tree in Sweden may not look particularly special, but it's more than 1,000 years old, so Vikings would have seen it in its youth!

OMMATOKOITA ELONGATA
This parasite is very picky—it feeds only on the eyes of Greenlandic sharks!

85% of these sharks are blinded in one or both eyes, but still hunt successfully!

SELF-DESTRUCTING TERMITES
In this termite species from French Guiana, elderly workers sacrifice themselves to help the colony. They grow pouches of toxic liquid, which they detonate onto their enemies!

HAIRY FROG
This Central African frog has a trick up its sleeve... or inside its feet, in fact. It can deliberately break the bones of its feet and push them outward to create claws.

BLUE WHALE
This whopping whale can eat up to 7,900 pounds (3,600 kg) per day—that's the largest appetite of any living animal.

Tiny krill make up the majority of its diet—it can digest 1.5 million of these crustaceans on a good day! The whale captures thousands at a time in its mouth before releasing the water surrounding them and then swallowing.

MIMIC OCTOPUS   This master of disguise can replicate at least 15 species, including lionfish, flatfish, flounder, sea jelly, sea sponge, and sea snake.

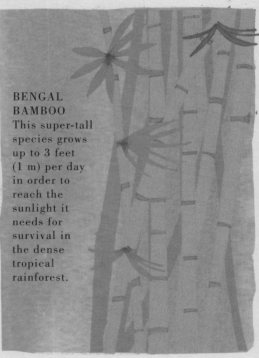

SPOTTED SALAMANDER
This surprising animal uses photosynthesis to extract energy from sunlight. Green algae inside its skin allow it to have this highly unusual property.

GIANT PANDA
Giant pandas know exactly what they like to eat—99% of their diet is bamboo!

BENGAL BAMBOO
This super-tall species grows up to 3 feet (1 m) per day in order to reach the sunlight it needs for survival in the dense tropical rainforest.

CAMEL
From its closable nostrils to its large, flat feet, the camel has an impressive array of desert adaptations.

RAFFLESIA
This plant produces the world's largest flower— it's 3 feet (1 m) across! It smells like rotten flesh, so it's called "corpse flower" or "meat flower" in local languages.

SAGUARO (CACTUS)
The saguaro grows extremely slowly, and may only begin sprouting "arms" after 75 years. But when it is finally ready to bloom, the flowers last for less than a day!

AFRICAN BULLFROG
This clever amphibian can hibernate underground in a mucus sac during dry seasons until the next rainfall. It can wait for several years!

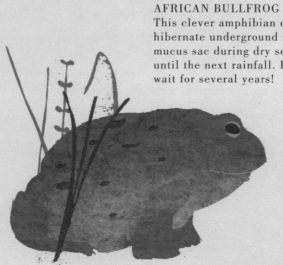

DIVING BELL SPIDER
Surfacing for air once a day, the world's only underwater spider will then use a bubble to supply itself with oxygen.

Super Survivalists

Species with extreme adaptations are known as extremophiles, and they love living life on the edge —inhabiting places that others steer well clear of. Some are incredibly tough and can withstand conditions that would be lethal to most life forms; all are amazingly interesting.

BACTERIA

Bacteria are made of single cells and are only about 0.00004 inches (1,000 mm) long. They can live at a huge range of temperatures, from ice to hot springs, and can even live in radioactive waste. Most bacteria are useful—gut bacteria produce vitamins and help people (and animals) digest their food, and bacteria in the roots help legumes (plants in the pea and bean family) get nitrogen out of the soil, which helps them to grow.

SILENE STENOPHYLLA

This delicate plant may not look particularly hardy, but it has grown from seeds that are 32,000 years old, which is a record by a huge margin. Once upon a time, a Siberian squirrel buried the seeds but never came back for them, and permafrost preserved the seeds alongside mammoth bones and other prehistoric material until scientists dug them up and managed to germinate the plants.

MOSS... AND OTHER ANTARCTIC PLANT LIFE

Algae, moss, and lichen are the main inhabitants of Antarctica. They can all survive with minimal warmth, sunlight, moisture, and nutrients. Mosses often anchor themselves to rocks to prevent themselves from being blown away, and to extract moisture. There are even two flowering plants that thrive in Antarctica—Antarctic hairgrass and Antarctic pearlwort. Both have been creeping further south due to warming temperatures!

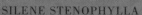

COCKROACHES

Considered as pests in some parts of the world and pets in others, these insects have been around since the age of the dinosaurs. They can go without food for six weeks, and when they do eat, they can survive on items such as glue and leather. Special bacteria in their guts help to create the amino acids they require, so it doesn't really matter if a cockroach doesn't have a naturally nutritious meal. Finally, they can survive *without their heads* for more than a week, until they starve or dry out!

TARDIGRADES

Perhaps the ultimate survivor is the tiny tardigrade, a microscopic creature less than 0.04 inches (1 mm) in size. It can be found in Antarctic ice, in the deep-sea, and in scorching deserts. It can survive in the vacuum of space, can be super-heated and super-cooled with no ill effects, and can be bombarded with radiation a million times stronger than that which would kill a human. In short, this is the most extreme of all the extremophiles!

Unsung Earthlings

There are a handful of species whose actions and interactions mold the planet into Earth as we know it. A little undersized and often overlooked, the following four species are the superstars of these unsung Earthlings.

BEES
These tiny workers help put food on our tables. They pollinate plants from apples to broccoli and from onions to almonds, allowing them to make seeds and reproduce. Without bees, many animal species would have a food crisis. Not only that, but up to 90% of wildflowers depend on bees for pollination, so without bees, the planet would suffer a catastrophic loss of biodiversity.

PLANKTON
What plankton lack in size, they make up for in numbers: the largest specimens are less than half an inch long, but there are billions of trillions of them altogether. They are divided into the plant-like phytoplankton, which extract energy from the Sun via photosynthesis. and the animal-like zooplankton. The phytoplankton produce approximately half of the world's oxygen, which is important for all other life forms.

BATS
Bees are not the only pollinators! Bats are crucial agents in the process, too, and are vital for seed dispersal. Simply put, entire ecosystems rely on the input of this flying mammal. It's lucky, then, that bats number in the millions. In fact, one in five mammals is a bat, which makes them one of the most successful types of animal on Earth.

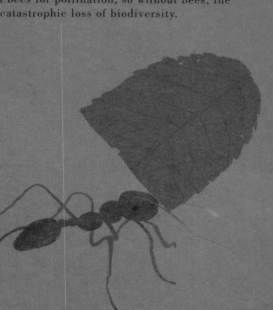

ANTS
Earthworms get most of the credit for churning up organic material to help form soil, and also for churning up existing soil, which releases vital nutrients for plant growth. But ants are much more active in carrying out this job, and are much more effective, too. They are the unsung tillers of the Earth.

FUNGI
Fungi act as nature's recyclers, processing organic material into a form that can be used again. Also, it was fungi that first allowed plants to move out of the oceans and onto the land, so these unglamorous heroes have helped to mold the planet into the place we know today.

PALAEOZOIC ERA (542–252 MYA)

Following the Hadean (4600–4000 MYA), Archean (4000–2500 MYA),
and Proterozoic eras (2500–542 MYA), the Palaeozoic was a time of explosion of life.

**CAMEROCERAS
(470–440 MYA)**
Growing up to 20 feet (6 m)
long, this early relative of
octopuses and squids was
the top predator of its time.

**TRILOBITE
(520–250 MYA)**
One of the most
successful creatures.
Found in oceans for more
than 270 million years.

**MEGANEUROPSIS
(300–260 MYA)**
This giant dragonfly had a
wingspan of 28 inches (71 cm)
—more than 4 times bigger
than the largest species alive.

**BRONTOSCORPIO
(420–360 MYA)**
Measuring up to 39 inches
(99 cm), this early scorpion
proved that gigantism was not
limited to the skies.

**DIMETRODON
(295–272 MYA)**
Not a dinosaur, mammal,
or reptile, but shared some
similarities with all groups.

**PTERODACTYLUS
(151– 148 MYA)**
"Winged finger" is an
example of a pterosaur
("winged lizard")—
the first vertebrates to
achieve powered flight.

**ARCHAEOPTERYX
(151–148 MYA)**
This dinosaur's name
means "ancient wing," and
it represents a transition
between dinosaurs and
modern birds.

A NOTE ON NUMBERS
MYA is short for
Million Years Ago.
The figures provided
on these pages are
scientists' best
estimates, though exact
figures are impossible
to know, and these
estimates could change
with new discoveries
and research.

**COMPSOGNATHUS
(145–140 MYA)**
Not all dinosaurs were big—this little
herbivore was the size of a chicken!

**MICRORAPTOR
(125–122 MYA)**
Tinier still was the "small robber,"
which was the size of a blackbird.

*Cretaceous Period
(144–65 MYA)*

In this relatively warm climate, dinosaurs continued to thrive,
along with pterosaurs (flying reptiles) and pliosaurs (large marine
reptiles). However, a massive extinction event ended this period.

Prehistoric
PLANET

Although the age of the dinosaurs ended long ago, you
might be surprised to learn that less time separates us
from T. Rex than separated T. Rex from Stegosaurus!
By taking a march through prehistoric time, you will
see that not all dinosaurs lived shoulder to shoulder
—very far from it.

**ANKYLOSAURUS
(74–67 MYA)**
A heavily-armored
herbivore with bony
plates, spines, and
a whip-like tail.

MESOZOIC ERA (252–65 MYA)

This era was the time of the dinosaurs, and is divided into three periods: Triassic, Jurassic, and Cretaceous.

Triassic Period (252–205 MYA)

The first dinosaurs evolved in the Triassic Period, and they started out small, with larger species developing toward the end of this time period.

EORAPTOR
(228–220 MYA)
Eoraptor was a light, small, and fast lizard-hipped dinosaur—one of the earliest dinosaurs on Earth.

PISANOSAURUS
(227–221 MYA)
A small, bird-hipped dinosaur, which would have been running alongside its lizard-hipped cousin, Eoraptor.

PLATEOSAURUS
(210–204 MYA)
One of the earliest examples of a big dinosaur, this 23-foot (7-m) creature's name means "broad lizard."

Jurassic Period (205–144 MYA)

Lush rainforests developed, supporting all sorts of life. Dinosaurs dominated the land and pterosaurs ruled the skies, but early lizards, mammals, and birds evolved, too.

STEGOSAURUS
(156–144 MYA)
This heavily-armored herbivore had a famously small brain.

ALLOSAURUS
(156–144 MYA)
This large dinosaur grew to about 33 feet (10 m) in length. Its name means "other lizard."

APATOSAURUS
(154–145 MYA)
Weighing up to 50 tons, this is one of the heaviest creatures of all time.

TRICERATOPS
(67–65 MYA)
Famous herbivore with three horns and a huge headcrest.

TYRANNOSAURUS REX
(67–65 MYA)
The top predator of its time, and one of the largest carnivores Earth has ever seen.

EXTINCTION EVENT

Almost three quarters of the Earth's plant and animal species became extinct in a short space of time, including all remaining dinosaurs. One theory is that a large asteroid hit the planet, creating dust clouds that blocked sunlight, disrupting photosynthesis and affecting the entire food chain.

10,000BC

At the end of the last Ice Age, humans shared their territory with an array of large mammals, most of which died out in a mass extinction event. It was around this time that man began farming, leading to a more settled existence.

ELASMOTHERIUM ("thin plate beast")
This giant rhinoceros was as big as a mammoth and had an enormous horn, giving him a unicorn-esque appearance.

WOOLLY MAMMOTH
Covered in shaggy fur, the woolly mammoth was ideally suited to cold conditions. Recent findings show that an isolated population existed on Wrangel Island in the Arctic Ocean until 2,500BC.

GLYPTODON ("grooved tooth")
A relative of the modern armadillo, this prehistoric beast grew as large as some cars!

MEGATHERIUM ("great beast")
This giant sloth measured 13 feet (4 m) tall when standing upright, and would have towered above early humans.

SMILODON ("knife tooth")
Often known as the saber-tooth tiger, this fierce predator weighed 440 pounds (200 kg) and sported canine teeth that were 7 inches (18 cm) long.

CAVE PAINTING
The earliest known cave paintings date back 40,000 years. Many scenes depict animals and hunting. Examples from 10,000BC are particularly well preserved.

DOMESTICATED CROPS
Farming food crops allowed humans to live more settled lives. Among the first crops domesticated were gourds, peas, and wheat.

VESSEL
Early drinking vessels were made from gourds, clay... and even human skulls!

DOMESTICATED GOAT
Humans not only learned how to farm crops, but they also domesticated animals. Goats provided these early farmers with milk, wool, and meat.

Earth REGIONS

*"I dream of our vast deserts, of our forests,
of all our great wildernesses."*

~ Nelson Mandela

The richness of Earth is in its variety — on a tour of
the globe an explorer may encounter lush, tropical
rainforests, deep and mysterious oceans, dry and
dusty deserts, and frigid, frozen poles. In addition
to the usual environments and habitats, we also take
a peek at cold-weather rainforests, deep-sea sulphur
vents, islands of all shapes and sizes, and Earth's most
extreme regions, which defy ordinary classification.

intertidal zone

This region is the transition zone between land and water. When the tide is in, the area is covered in water, and when the tide is out, land is exposed. Sea stars, as well as crabs and other small crustaceans, make their home in this environment.

WHAT CAUSES TIDES?

The gravity of the Moon attracts ocean water, causing it to bulge out in the direction of the Moon. This results in a high tide.

epipelagic zone

The surface layer of the ocean extends to a depth of 660 feet (200 m). Sunlight is strong here, and temperatures in this zone can vary widely between the tropics and the poles.

SEA ANEMONE AND CLOWNFISH

The sea anemone provides a safe home for the clownfish. The clownfish, in turn, protects the sea anemone from predators, and provides it with nutrients in the form of its waste.

mesopelagic zone

Sunlight reaches down to about 3,300 feet (1,000 m), so this second layer of the ocean is often called the twilight zone.

CYCLOTHONE

This little fish is the most common vertebrate on Earth, yet it is not widely known by people outside of the scientific and fishing communities.

FLABBY WHALEFISH

This fish appears bright red when brought to the surface, yet it cannot be seen by predators and prey as red coloration is invisible at such depths.

bathypelagic zone

Known as the midnight zone because no sunlight reaches these depths, the third zone of the ocean extends from 3,300 to 13,000 feet (1,000 to 4,000 m). Despite being a cold and dark place, life is super-abundant.

GULPER EEL

Also known as the pelican eel, this deep-sea fish has a huge hinged jaw, enabling it to catch many fish in one scoop.

SEA SPIDER

Some long-legged sea spiders have been spotted walking along the super-deep seafloor.

Oceans

Life on Earth originated in the oceans, and an incredibly diverse web of life still exists in the marine environment today. 99% of the Earth's living area is underwater, but only 10% of the oceans have been properly explored, meaning there are countless species, particularly in the darkest depths, which have never met man's gaze.

We divide the oceans into five vertical zones, from the uppermost 660 feet (200 m) to the deepest ocean trenches.

abyssopelagic zone

The word "abyss" literally means "bottomless," and this zone is largely unexplored. One study revealed 898 species in an area about half the size of a tennis court, and most of these species were new to science!

Deep-sea dives

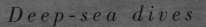

Deepest dive by bird......................690 feet (210 m)
Deepest free-dive by human..........702 feet (214 m)
Deepest dive by whale.................9,816 feet (2,992 m)
Deepest dive by submersible
(diving machine)........................35,797 feet (10,911 m)

PLANKTON
These miniature creatures support the entire ocean food chain. About 1 million plankton species were recorded during the Tara Oceans expedition, which took more than two years.

SEA BIRDS
There are many flying visitors to the ocean environment—some can dive to depths of 200 feet (60 m) in search of their favorite food.

HAMMERHEAD SHARK
Wide-set eyes help the hammerhead shark to scan the ocean for prey, so the oddly-shaped head makes it a better hunter!

DAGGERTOOTH
A vicious eel that lives in shallow waters, this species can grow up to 6.6 feet (2 m).

CUTTLEFISH
The eight-armed cuttlefish has three hearts and green-blue blood. Some species can grow as big as a rugby ball.

CHAIN CATSHARK (OR DOGFISH)
This little shark is less than 10 inches (50 cm) long and has skin that can glow bright green!

SWORDFISH
With a top speed of 50 miles per hour (80 kph), few fish can outswim this pointy-billed predator.

ANGLERFISH
In the murkiness of the deep sea, fish are attracted to the glowing light on the end of the female's "fishing pole." Her super-sharp teeth then chomp down on those lured too close!

GIANT SQUID & COLOSSAL SQUID
With giant squids growing to 43 feet (13 m) in length and their colossal cousins thought to reach 46 feet (14 m), these eight-armed giants have long been mistaken for sea monsters!

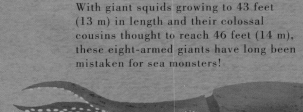

BLACK SWALLOWER
A balloon-like stomach allows the black swallower to swallow fish 10 times as heavy as itself, and twice as long!

GIANT TUBE WORM
These worms anchor themselves to rocks on the seafloor.

In warm waters, they achieve giant size in a couple of years, whereas in cold waters it can take centuries.

SEA CUCUMBER
When attacked, this creature can do something very unusual —it can shoot out *its own insides* to fight off predators! Its stomach and other organs will soon grow back.

hadalpelagic zone
Named after Hades, the underworld in Greek mythology, this is the deepest of the five vertical zones and extends to around 6.8 miles (11 km) beneath the surface. There are 46 "hadal" (super-deep) habitats worldwide, mostly concentrated in the Pacific, where plate tectonics have created huge ocean trenches.

NOT TO SCALE
If the ocean layers were shown to scale in this diagram, keeping the top layer unchanged, the page would need to extend 7.2 feet (2.2 m) to reach the bottom of the hadalpelagic zone!

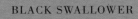

Islands

Islands are important: they make up about a sixth of the Earth's land area, and a quarter of all countries are island nations. Depending on what's considered an island and what's merely an "islet," there are up to 20,000 of them in our oceans, lakes, and rivers. Due to their isolation, many species have evolved differently to their mainland counterparts, as Charles Darwin came to realize on his voyage to the Galapagos.

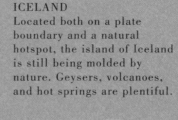
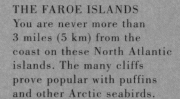

GREENLAND
85% of the world's largest island is covered in ice, so the 60,000 islanders live on settlements hugging the coast. There are no roads to connect towns and villages.

The colorful capital, Nuuk

ICELAND
Located both on a plate boundary and a natural hotspot, the island of Iceland is still being molded by nature. Geysers, volcanoes, and hot springs are plentiful.

The birth of Surtsey, 1963

THE FAROE ISLANDS
You are never more than 3 miles (5 km) from the coast on these North Atlantic islands. The many cliffs prove popular with puffins and other Arctic seabirds.

Puffins outnumber people!

GOLDEN MANTELLA
This little frog comes in two types —yellow and red, both of which are endangered. Like 99% of Madagascan frogs, it can be found only on the island.

BAOBAB
These thick-trunked trees are known as renala in the local language, meaning "mother of the forest." In the west of the island is the Avenue of the Baobabs—a unique spot on Earth.

"TRAVELER'S TREE"
This enormous fan-like tree is officially known as *Ravenala madagascariensis*, but we'll stick with traveler's tree, as that's slightly less of a mouthful.

MADAGASCAR
Separated from the mainland for 88 million years, there's been plenty of time for life to evolve in unique ways on this tropical island. More than 90% of species can be found nowhere else, including lemurs, almost 1,000 species of orchids, more than 100 types of fish, more than half of the world's chameleon species, and around 300 frog species. Because of this astonishing richness, Madagascar is sometimes referred to as the world's eighth continent.

GIANT COUA
Related to the cuckoo, this big bird is almost double the size of its mainland cousins.

RAINBOW PANTHER CHAMELEON
This colorful master of disguise can be found in the central tropical rainforest regions...if you look very closely!

KIRIBATI
The average elevation of this Pacific island nation is less than 6.5 feet (2 m), so rising sea levels are a real danger. The islands are the tips of underwater volcanoes.

SINGAPORE
The city-state of Singapore has not only grown upward via skyscrapers, but it has grown outward, too, by piling sand offshore to build new land. 22% of its land area is man-made!

NEW GUINEA
New Guinea is home to more than 850 languages, making it the most linguistically diverse place on the planet. Many tribes still practice ancient traditions.

SOCOTRA
Home to many strange species including the desert rose and the dragon blood tree, Socotra has been termed the most alien-looking place on Earth!

Traditional house

SkyPark: pool with a view!

A Huli "wigman"

The desert rose

N O R T H

ELEPHANT BIRD
Standing more than 10 feet (3 m) tall, the flightless elephant bird would have towered over humans. Adults weighed up to half a ton, and their eggs alone weighed 22 pounds (10 kg)! The species is thought to have been hunted to extinction in the 1800s.

ORCHID
There are almost 1,000 species of this delicate flower, 850 of which are only found on the island.

LEMUR
Madagascar is home to all 50 of the world's lemur species.

Rainforests

In simple terms, rainforests are places with a lot of rain and many trees. They are teeming with life—more than half the world's species are concentrated in rainforests, despite these habitats only taking up 6% of the Earth's surface. They used to stretch to 14%, but human activity has resulted in more than half of the world's rainforests being cut down, and the remaining forests are under severe threat.

Emergent Layer

LAYERS
Rainforests can be divided into distinct layers ranging from the emergent layer to the forest floor. Because the forest is so dense, rain can take 10 minutes to reach the floor.

Amazon Rainforest

Stretching across nine countries, this is the largest tropical rainforest in the world. Its 400 billion trees help to produce about 20% of the world's oxygen. It boasts an extraordinary variety of life, including 40,000 plant species, 1,300 bird species, 3,000 fish species, 430 mammal species, and around 2.5 million insect species, a handful of which you can see in the picture:

1. HARPY EAGLE – world's largest and most powerful eagle.

2. THREE-TOED SLOTH – so slow that algae grows on its fur.

3. SMOKY JUNGLE FROG – known to eat its own tadpoles!

4. POISON DART FROG – only 2 inches (5 cm) long but can kill 10 men.

5. CAPUCHIN MONKEY – eats fruit, nuts, insects, and frogs.

6. BOA CONSTRICTOR – super-long snake with a deadly grip.

7. JAGUAR – one of the top predators of the rainforest.

8. CAPYBARA – world's largest rodent; weighs up to 150 pounds (70 kg).

9. LEAFCUTTER ANTS – mini farmers; use leaves to feed fungus.

10. AMAZONIAN TAPIR – among the largest South American mammals.

Congo Rainforest

The Congo is home to the second biggest rainforest in the world, and in places it is so dense that only 1% of sunlight reaches the floor. It's the only place in the world with all four sub-species of gorilla (mountain, western lowland, eastern lowland, and cross river), and it is also home to bonobos (mankind's closest living relative) and the okapi, which looks like a cross between a zebra and a giraffe.

Canopy

Understory

Shrub layer

Floor

Temperate Rainforests

When you think of rainforests, you probably don't think of Japan, Scotland, or New Zealand. But these places are all home to temperate rainforests, meaning they have a lot of trees and a lot of rain, but are much colder than tropical rainforests. This picture shows fiordland crested penguins, which nest in the trees of New Zealand. Yep, penguins in a rainforest — it's absolutely true!

Sumatran Rainforest

The words *wild* and *life* could not be more appropriate on this Indonesian island. It's the only place in the world where you can see tigers, orangutans, elephants, and rhinos together in the wild. However, due to deforestation, poaching, and a growing human population, some experts think that the entire rainforest could disappear in 20 years if we don't protect this precious ecosystem.

Poles

Located at the ends of the planet, the poles are incredibly cold, and species need clever adaptations to survive here. Due to the way the seasons work, each pole gets plunged into darkness in winter, with no sunlight at all for several months at the absolute extremes.

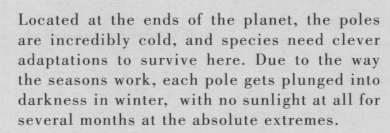

ALBATROSS
The albatross can glide and soar for hours without flapping its huge wings. It eats fish and squid and drinks salt water.

ARCTIC TERN
This super-commuter travels all the way from the Arctic to the Antarctic each year—a round trip of more than 50,000 miles (80,000 km)!

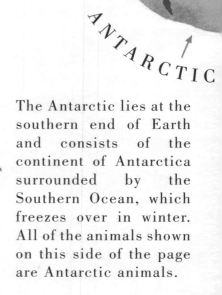

ANTARCTIC

CRABEATER SEAL
Despite their name, crabeater seals eat krill rather than crabs! They are the most common seal species, and millions can be found around the Antarctic coast.

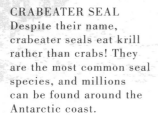

ELEPHANT SEAL
Elephant seals can weigh up to 8,800 pounds (4 tonnes)...which is as much as an elephant! However, their name doesn't come from their size—it comes from their unusual trunk-like inflatable snouts.

PENGUINS
There are 17 species of penguin in total, all living in the southern hemisphere, and many living in the waters around Antarctica. The emperor penguin (shown on the left) is the largest species—adults can weigh up to 88 pounds (40 kg). Slightly smaller is the king penguin (in the middle), and the gentoo penguin (right, pronounced JEN-too) has the longest tail of any penguin species.

The Antarctic lies at the southern end of Earth and consists of the continent of Antarctica surrounded by the Southern Ocean, which freezes over in winter. All of the animals shown on this side of the page are Antarctic animals.

BLUE WHALE
This is the largest animal to have ever lived on Earth. Its tongue weighs as much as an elephant, and its heart weighs as much as a car.

HUMPBACK WHALE
Humpbacks feed in polar waters in the summer, then migrate to subtropical regions to breed in the winter.

KRILL
This tiny species plays a huge part in the ocean food chain. Krill are found in every ocean on Earth.

SNOWY OWL
This bird is a patient hunter, and uses its excellent eyesight and white camouflage to catch its favorite prey: lemmings.

REINDEER
Both males and females have long antlers. The reindeer feed mainly on lichen and have an excellent sense of smell to sniff out food sources under the snow, then use their hooves to dig until they have located their meal.

ARCTIC

The Arctic lies at the northern end of the globe. There is no land at the North Pole, but a large ice sheet covers the cold ocean waters. Parts of North America, Europe, and Asia extend into Arctic regions, supporting large mammals.

MUSK OX
This giant plant-eater has two layers of fur to help it survive the long Arctic winters.

POLAR BEAR
Although feared by many Arctic animals, less than 2% of a polar bear's hunting attempts are thought to be successful!

ARCTIC FOX
The well-camouflaged Arctic fox sometimes follows a polar bear and scavenges on leftovers if its own hunting trips are unsuccessful.

WALRUS
These gentle giants use their long tusks to break through the ice, and to climb out of the sea and onto an iceshelf.

PUFFIN
Orange-beaked puffins are superb fliers and hunters—they can flap their wings 400 times per minute, fly 55 miles per hour (88 kph), and dive 200 feet (60 m) underwater to catch their meal.

ARCTIC HARE
Groups of up to 100 animals have been known to huddle together to keep warm in extreme conditions.

ORCA
Also known as killer whales, orcas use their massive teeth to hunt animals such as fish, squid, and sea lions in the water, and even jump into the air to grab low-flying sea birds. They are found in all oceans, but particularly thrive in Arctic waters.

NARWHAL
This mysterious whale species with a super-long tusk usually avoids human observation. They live in pods of 10–100 individuals, and consume squid, fish, and shrimp.

JACKAL
Related to wolves and dogs, jackals have light fur, which provides camouflage in desert and semi-desert environments.

OSTRICH
The largest and fastest bird in the world lives in deserts and savannas. Like a camel, the ostrich has long eyelashes to keep sand out.

ADDAX
This type of antelope rarely drinks water —it gets most of its moisture directly from plants. It can smell rainfall from miles away and so knows where new grasses will sprout.

TERMITES
Termites construct air-conditioned towers of earth, which house up to 2 million individuals. They work 24 hours a day and never sleep! In Africa, a termite queen can lay up to 30,000 eggs a day, so it's no surprise that the world is teeming with termites!

SCARAB BEETLE
Scarabs come in 30,000 species and are found in most habitats—not just deserts. However, only in Egypt have they had such high status that man actually worshipped them!

JERBOA
This little rodent doesn't drink water at all, getting all of its moisture from plants instead. Like the fennec fox, its large ears help it to maintain a cool temperature, and it can jump high and run fast to escape predators.

Deserts

About a third of the Earth's land surface is classified as desert because it receives very little moisture. Our classic image is of sandy subtropical deserts, but even in the Sahara, desert dunes account for a fraction of the total area—plant life is usually able to take root and anchor sand and soil to prevent dune formation in all but the most barren and inhospitable parts. Even here, life still goes on, with animals displaying remarkable adaptations to their environment.

DORCAS GAZELLE
Although it drinks when it finds water, this desert-adapted gazelle could survive its entire life without drinking water directly!

DUNE FORMATION
The wind sculpts dunes of sand, and a landscape can be transformed overnight. One of the most common dune types is crescent-shaped, with sand piling up on one side, with the other side shielded from the wind.

Wind direction

CAMEL
The camel's many adaptations include long eyelashes and closable nostrils to keep sand out, wide feet to prevent sinking in sand, and, of course, the hump, which stores energy as fat.

SANDFISH
The sandfish is a type of lizard that dives into loose sand and "swims" through dunes to keep cool and to avoid predators.

DESERT MONITOR LIZARD
Some like it hot—this lizard becomes sluggish and doesn't function well if its body temperature drops too low!

FENNEC FOX
The super-large ears radiate heat away and help to keep the foxes cool. They have hairy feet to prevent burning on sand, and they can go for long periods without water.

DEATHSTALKER SCORPION
As its name suggests, this scorpion is exremely dangerous, possessing the strongest venom of any scorpion species. Similar to the desert monitor lizard, its body systems are designed to run at high temperatures, and it is over-cooling that presents more of a problem to the scorpion!

Deserts of the World

Deserts are not only located near the equator—they are found on all seven continents. Our classic image of a desert is a hot, sandy subtropical desert such as the Sahara, but this is only one of the four major types.

Subtropical desert
Cool coastal desert
Cold winter desert
Polar desert

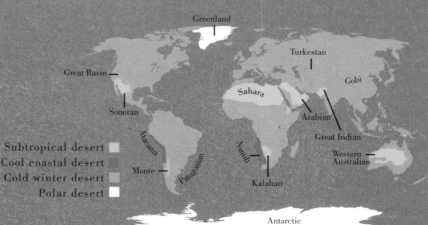

Greenland

Turkestan

Great Basin

Gobi

Sahara

Sonoran

Arabian

Great Indian

Atacama

Namib

Western Australian

Monte

Patagonian

Kalahari

Antarctic

Extreme Earth

Far from the hotspots of human habitation, some record-setting locations can be found. These are the Earth's extremities—the highest, lowest, hottest, coldest—and you will soon see that one cold-spot is in fact a hotspot for world records.

EVEREST
At 29,029 feet (8,848 m), Mount Everest is famously the highest peak above sea level. But it isn't the *tallest* mountain, and nor is it the point furthest from the center of the Earth.

CHIMBORAZO
The peak of this Ecuadorian mountain is further from the center of the Earth than the peak of Mount Everest! That's because the Earth has a slight bulge at the equator. Despite this fact, Everest is almost 6,600 feet (2,000 m) higher above sea level.

COLDEST RECORDED TEMPERATURE
In 1983, a temperature of −128.6°F (−89.2°C) was recorded at Vostok Station in Antarctica. Modern satellite data suggests the surrounding mountains experience even lower readings.

HIGHEST RECORDED TEMPERATURE
In the summer of 1913, Furnace Creek in Death Valley, California, experienced a temperature of 134°F (56.7°C)—a sweltering world record.

SEA LEVEL

WETTEST PLACE
The north Indian village of Mawsynram receives almost 39 feet (12 m) of rainfall per year, making it among the wettest places on the planet.

DRIEST PLACE
It hasn't officially rained in 14 million years in the McMurdo Dry Valleys of Antarctica, though some snow sometimes gets blown over from nearby hills. Almost no life can survive here without the essential ingredient of water.

K2
Standing 28,251 feet (8,611 m) above sea level, K2 is the second highest mountain in the world. It sits on the border between Pakistan and China and is extremely challenging to climb.

GANGKHAR PUENSUM
This peak that rises 24,836 feet (7,570 m) lies in the tiny kingdom of Bhutan and is the highest unclimbed mountain the world. The Bhutanese government bans mountaineering because it considers mountains as the place of gods rather than men, so it is highly unlikely to be climbed in the foreseeable future.

HIGHEST WATERFALL
Water at the Angel Falls in Venezuela experiences freefall for 3,212 feet (979 m). This is 15 times the height of the Niagara Falls, and it takes the water about 14 seconds to reach the pool at the base.

BIGGEST, OLDEST & DEEPEST LAKE
A fifth of the world's freshwater can be found in Lake Baikal, Siberia—its size is bigger than some seas! It's also home to the world's only freshwater seal, making this a remarkably record-breaking body of water.

KILIMANJARO
This is the highest peak in Africa and the highest free-standing mountain in the world, which means it's not part of a chain. Its peak is 19,341 feet (5,895 m) above sea level.

MAUNA KEA
Measuring an astonishing 33,476 feet (10,204 m) from top to bottom, this ancient Hawaiian volcano is by far the tallest mountain in the world. But it isn't as high above the ground as Everest—that's because almost 60% of its height lies under the ocean.

DEEPEST NATURAL HOLE
The Mariana Trench in the Pacific Ocean plunges almost 6.8 miles (11 km) below sea level. Even at this depth, microbial life thrives in the cold, dark waters of this super-deep hole.

HIGHEST BIODIVERSITY
Tropical rainforests host the greatest variety of life, and two particular hotspots vying for the biodiversity record are the Brazilian Amazon and the Panamanian Rainforest. Because many species remain undiscovered, it is extremely difficult to pick a definitive winner here!

LOWEST BIODIVERSITY
Antarctica is the title-holder yet again! The largest permanent animal inhabitants on this frozen continent are tiny tardigrades—nowhere else is a microscope needed to see an entire habitat's biggest creatures.

Otherworldly Environments

Life is very adaptable and can be found thriving in some incredibly hostile and unlikely environments....

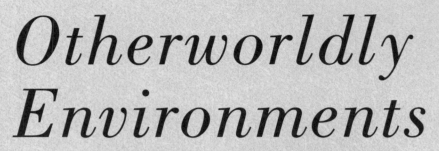

HIGH
The Himalayan jumping spider lives at altitudes up to 22,000 feet (6,700 m)—higher than any other species. There is nothing this high for it to hunt, but fortunately the wind blows frozen insects up the mountain!

HOT
The Yellowstone hot springs support a life form called archaea—one of the most basic forms, but so poorly understood that it wasn't classified as life until the 1970s. It can survive in extreme temperatures, so it's thought to have thrived in Earth's primordial phase.

DRY
Death Valley is one of the hottest places on Earth, so it would seem an unlikely place to look for fish. However, it used to be a massive lake, and a small population of Devil's hole pupfish still manage an existence in a pool of water in a crack in the rocks.

DEEP
Hardy nematode worms have been found among solid rock in mine shafts 1.9 miles (3 km) beneath the Earth's surface. Water, heat, pressure, darkness, and lack of nutrients make this home very impressive!

DARK
Life as we knew it needed sunlight for photosynthesis at the beginning of the food chain. But around some deep-sea vents, ecosystems have been discovered which use *chemosynthesis* instead—drawing energy directly from the Earth's minerals. One of the most common life-forms in such environments is the ringworm.

The
HUMAN
Planet

We do not inherit the Earth from our ancestors,
but borrow it from our children."

~ Native American proverb

Humans are the only large land animal to have colonized all corners of the globe. We are also the only species to have domesticated other plant and animal species, and in doing so, we have drastically altered the landscape of the planet. The modern planet therefore unquestionably has a human dimension, and in this section we explore the human migration story, cities and towns, world wonders, and different cultures from around the globe, before pausing to consider threats to our planet and what we can do to create a sustainable future.

1,200

25,000

40,000

100,000

70,000

A WORLD OF HOMININS
The map shows that *Homo erectus* existed in Africa, Asia, and parts of Europe. *Homo neanderthalensis* remains have been found in Europe, the Middle East, and western Asia. And *Homo sapiens* (that's us!) has colonized almost the entire globe—the numbers on the map by the yellow arrows represent the number of years ago that modern man reached a particular area.

WHERE MAN BEGAN
Homo sapiens first evolved in Africa, and thrived on the continent for about 100,000 years before venturing to other parts of the world.

200,000

1500

50,000

The
HUMAN STORY

We have many ancestors who lived in the world before us. Humans and human-like creatures are called hominins, and one of the earliest hominins was *Australopithecus* ("southern ape"), which became extinct about 2 million years ago. *Homo habilis* ("handy man") was among the earliest *Homo-* species, and *Homo erectus* ("upright man") showed significant development. *Homo neanderthalensis* lived until relatively recently, and our own species, *Homo sapiens* ("wise man"), has existed for about 200,000 years.

HOMO NEANDERTHALENSIS
This well-built species died out around 30,000 years ago. They were able to breed with *Homo sapiens*, and having *Homo neanderthalensis* ancestors has helped our immune systems.

HOMO ERECTUS
This successful branch of hominins—whose name means "upright man"—first emerged around 1.8 million years ago. They used tools, technology, and culture to hunt and gather food.

HOMO SAPIENS
Modern humans are the only surviving hominin species. Our species evolved about 200,000 years ago, and we have had an enormous impact on the planet through our interactions with other species.

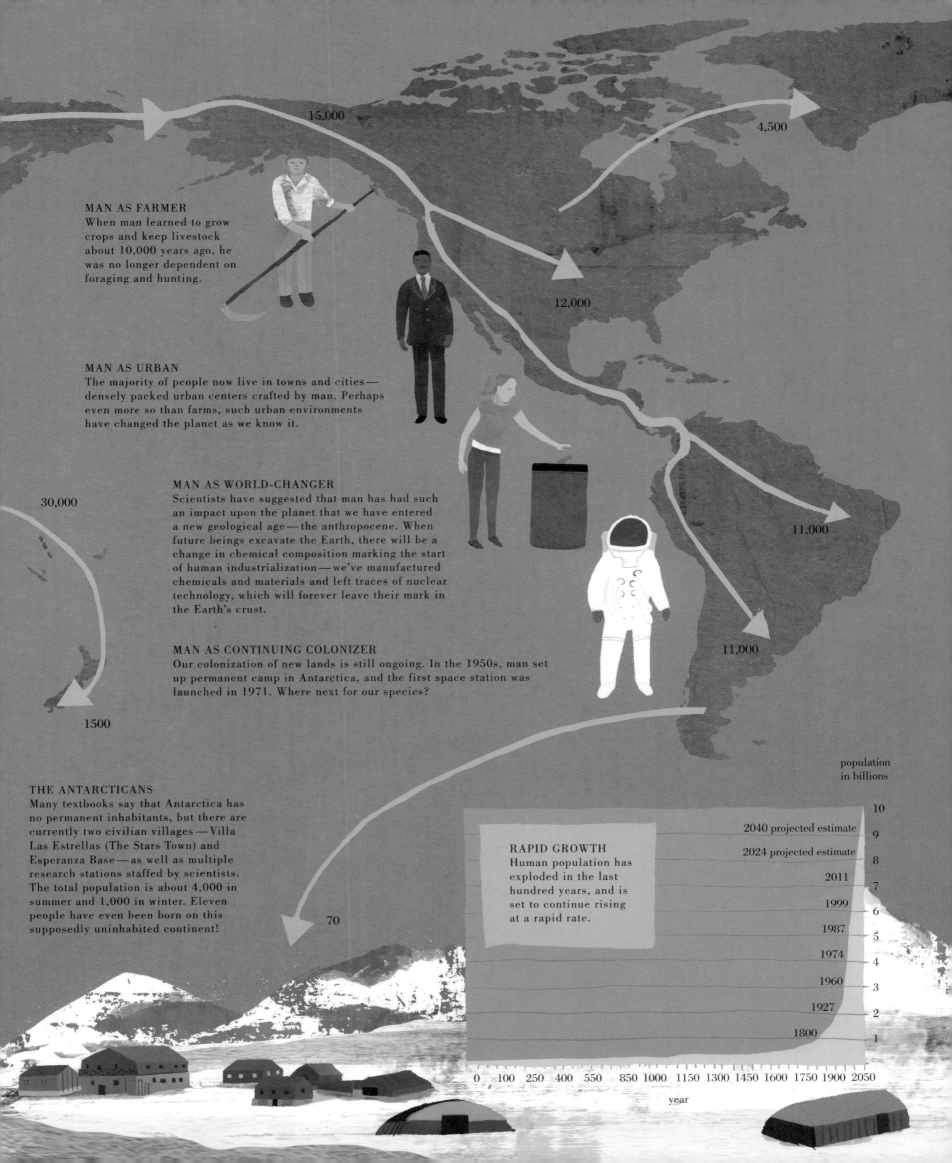

15,000

4,500

MAN AS FARMER
When man learned to grow crops and keep livestock about 10,000 years ago, he was no longer dependent on foraging and hunting.

12,000

MAN AS URBAN
The majority of people now live in towns and cities—densely packed urban centers crafted by man. Perhaps even more so than farms, such urban environments have changed the planet as we know it.

30,000

MAN AS WORLD-CHANGER
Scientists have suggested that man has had such an impact upon the planet that we have entered a new geological age—the anthropocene. When future beings excavate the Earth, there will be a change in chemical composition marking the start of human industrialization—we've manufactured chemicals and materials and left traces of nuclear technology, which will forever leave their mark in the Earth's crust.

11,000

MAN AS CONTINUING COLONIZER
Our colonization of new lands is still ongoing. In the 1950s, man set up permanent camp in Antarctica, and the first space station was launched in 1971. Where next for our species?

11,000

1500

THE ANTARCTICANS
Many textbooks say that Antarctica has no permanent inhabitants, but there are currently two civilian villages—Villa Las Estrellas (The Stars Town) and Esperanza Base—as well as multiple research stations staffed by scientists. The total population is about 4,000 in summer and 1,000 in winter. Eleven people have even been born on this supposedly uninhabited continent!

70

population in billions

10

2040 projected estimate
9

2024 projected estimate
8

RAPID GROWTH
Human population has exploded in the last hundred years, and is set to continue rising at a rapid rate.

2011
7

1999
6

1987
5

1974
4

1960
3

1927
2

1800
1

0   100   250   400   550   850 1000 1150 1300 1450 1600 1750 1900 2050

year

PARADE *of* PEOPLE

With around 200 countries, 7,000 languages, and tens of thousands of tribes, clans, and subgroups, human culture is incredibly varied. Feast your eyes on this collection of remarkable groups of people from around the globe, focusing especially on those where ancient traditions have continued.

GREENLANDIC
Greenlandic people live in a snowy-white environment, but have an extraordinarily colorful culture, reflected in their national costume, made from thick wool called *holmensklæde* ("island cloth").

ABORIGINAL, AUSTRALIA
There are more than 500 groups or tribes of aboriginal people in Australia, all of which have strong storytelling cultures, a deep respect for nature, and a belief system that allows them to live in harmony with their natural surroundings.

ASARO MUDMEN, PAPUA NEW GUINEA
Terrifying clay masks are worn by warriors, who have traditionally raided neighboring villages at night. Anyone who sees them in this disguise thinks they are from the evil spirit world.

TIBETAN
Living at high altitudes, Tibetans generally wear a thick *chuba*, which keeps out the cold. Dead bodies cannot be buried because frosty soil is unsuitable, so corpses are instead left to vultures in a "sky burial"!

MAASAI, KENYA & TANZANIA
The Maasai people count their wealth in cattle and children—it is best to have plenty of both! In order to become a warrior, young men have to prove themselves by killing a lion with a spear. This is perhaps the toughest "rite of passage" in the world.

NENETS, NORTHERN RUSSIA
The reindeer-herding Nenets people live on the Yamal Peninsula in Russia. *Yamal* means "the end of the world" in their language, and it's not difficult to see why. Also in the words of a herder: *"The reindeer is our home, our food, our warmth, and our transportation."*

TUAREG, NORTH AFRICA
The Tuareg people have been roaming the Sahara for as long as anyone can remember. Many still lead semi-nomadic lives, moving across the wilderness with their camels and livestock. Unusually, men wear veils, whereas women do not cover their faces.

DOGON, MALI
These West African people have a stilt-dancing festival, in which they imitate the graceful movements of the *tingetange*, a long-legged water bird. The dancers complete complex moves from high above the crowd.

KAZAKH EAGLE HUNTERS, MONGOLIA
In Western Mongolia, a small number of Kazakh people continue a tradition dating back centuries. They ride on horseback and train golden eagles to hunt foxes and hares. Such hunting partnerships between man and eagle can last a lifetime.

KAYAN, MYANMAR
It's traditional for Kayan women in Southeast Asia to wear brass rings around their necks. Over time, their shoulders shrink, giving the appearance of very extended necks. Unsurprisingly they are nicknamed "the giraffe people".

HULI WIGMEN, PAPUA NEW GUINEA
There are more than 850 tribes in Papua New Guinea, but the colorful Huli are often the stars of inter-tribal festivals called "sing sings" because of their amazing costumes.

MURSI, ETHIOPIA
It's fashionable in this tribe for young women to pierce the lower lip and then put a clay plate in the hole. Over time, the hole can expand to accommodate discs measuring 4.7 inches (12 cm) across!

SATERÉ-MAWÉ, AMAZON
Boys of this Amazonian tribe need to pass a painful test to become warriors. They must wear gloves containing bullet ants, which have the strongest sting in the insect world. Participants sometimes shake in agony for days afterward.

SUMO WRESTLERS, JAPAN
A special type of wrestling has been practiced in Japan for centuries. Huge, strong competitors train for many years to master the 88 techniques, but a typical bout lasts only seven seconds! These days, competitors come from around the world—it's not uncommon to see Hawaiian, Mongolian, and European wrestlers!

SENTINELESE, INDIA
These remote islanders have resisted almost all contact with outsiders. When a helicopter flew over to check on their well-being after a hurricane, tribesman pointed their bows and arrows at this potentially hostile flying machine!

Super Cities

In 2008, for the first time in history most people lived in cities and towns rather than in villages and the countryside. As our population continues to grow, cities will carry on spreading upward and outward, and more and more people will be attracted to these magnets of culture, finance, work, and play.

No two cities are alike, so hop on board for a whistlestop tour of a few of the finest examples of our modern urban world, from all six continents where cities have sprung up. Which ones would you most like to visit, and why?

LONDON
London is a mix of old and new, with historic Big Ben and Tower Bridge rubbing shoulders with newcomers such as The Shard and The Gherkin. One of the most famous residents is Queen Elizabeth II, who lives at Buckingham Palace.

NEW YORK
The Statue of Liberty has been greeting newcomers to the "Big Apple" since 1886, and NY is now one of the most diverse places on the planet. There are many highlights for visitors, including the Empire State Building, Manhattan's skyscrapers, Central Park, Times Square, and Madison Square Garden.

PARIS
Boasting amazing architecture, cultural curiosities, and delicious cuisine, it is no surprise that picturesque Paris is one of the most important and most visited cities in the world.

CAIRO
The mighty River Nile runs through the historic and splendid Egyptian capital. Just outside the city are the pyramids of Giza, but modern travelers are treated to a modern wonder, too— 2 million cars navigating a city originally designed for camel-based transportation!

TOKYO

By many measures, Tokyo is the biggest city on Earth, with a bustling center and suburbs extending into the surrounding plains. The underground trains are so crowded that people are employed to push travelers into tightly-packed train cars! Neon signs famously light the streets at night, and in spring there is another visual feast — it's the time of the cherry blossom. The sight is so beautiful that there's a special word for viewing and appreciating the bloom: *hanami*.

SYDNEY

About 20% of Australia's population lives in this coastal city, and citizens are known as Sydneysiders. Sydney Harbour Bridge has been standing since 1932, and the iconic Sydney Opera House followed in 1973. It took 14 years and 10,000 construction workers to complete this world-famous building.

ISTANBUL

Turkey's largest city sits at the crossroads between Europe and Asia, and there is a vibrant blend of East and West in the city's streets and architecture, from towering minarets to bubbling bathhouses. Locals and tourists alike are mesmerized by the beauty of the Blue Mosque and the bustle of the Grand Bazaar.

RIO DE JANEIRO

This Brazilian city on the Atlantic coast is one of the most visited spots in the southern hemisphere. It's famous not only for the statue of Christ the Redeemer, but also for its spectacular carnival. In 2016, people from around the world came to visit to watch the 31st summer Olympic Games, and the motto sums up the spirit of the city: *live your passion*.

HONG KONG

Hong Kong has twice as many skyscrapers as any other city, including one with a hole built into it to help dragons pass through safely! The city's name means fragrant harbor in Cantonese, the local language.

MASDAR

Designed to be a sustainable, environmentally friendly, self-sufficient eco-city in the desert of Abu Dhabi, plans are currently on hold for this project. Could this "city of the future" already be a thing of the past?

COUNTRIES and CONTINENTS

KING OF THE COASTLINES
Canada has by far the longest coastline of any country, thanks to its huge size and its many islands and inlets.

Greenland
(Denmark)

Alaska
(U.S.)

Iceland

Canada

Europe

Area: 3.9 million mi²
(10.2 million km²)
Population: 0.7 billion

Small in size but big in influence, Europe is home to around 50 countries, more than half of which belong to the European Union, which promotes greater trade and cooperation among members.

A NATION OF STATES
Consisting of 50 states plus the District of Columbia, the U.S. has a unique structure.

United States

Ireland · United Kingdom · Netherlands · Denmark · Norway · Sweden
Belgium · Germany
Luxembourg · Czech Rep. · Austria
France · Liechtenstein · Switzerland
Portugal · Spain · Monaco · Italy · Vatican City

North America

Area: 9.4 million mi²
(24.4 million km²)
Population: 0.5 billion

Stretching from the icy Arctic to the tropical Caribbean, this continent contains 23 countries and such treasures as Niagara Falls, the Statue of Liberty, and the Mayan temple city of Chichen Itza.

Mexico

Cuba
Bahamas

Belize
Jamaica
Honduras
Haiti
Dominican Republic
Saint Kitts and Nevis
Antigua and Barbuda
Dominica
St. Lucia
St. Vincent and the Grenadines
Barbados
Grenada
Trinidad and Tobago

Guatemala
El Salvador
Nicaragua
Costa Rica
Panama

Atlantic Ocean

Morocco
Western Sahara
Algeria
Lib
Mauritania
Mali
Niger
Cape Verde
Senegal
Gambia
Guinea-Bissau
Guinea
Sierra Leone
Liberia
Côte d'Ivoire
Burkina Faso
Ghana
Nigeria
Cameroon
Equatorial Guinea
São Tomé and Príncipe
Gabon

Colombia
Venezuela
Guyana
Suriname
French Guiana (France)
Ecuador
Peru

Pacific Ocean

Brazil
Brazil shares a border with every country in South America except Ecuador and Chile.

Africa

Area: 11.7 million mi²
(30.4 million km²)
Population: 1.0 billion

There are 54 countries in Africa, from Tunisia in the north to South Africa in the south. The continent contains deserts, rainforests, jungles, savannas, and plains.

Bolivia

South America

Area: 6.9 million mi²
(17.8 million km²)
Population: 0.4 billion

The continent is dominated geographically by Brazil, which takes up almost half of the area, but the smaller nations are important, too, and are hotspots for tourism, culture, and industry. South America is home to the Andes mountains as well as the Amazon Rainforest.

Paraguay

Chile

Uruguay
Argentina

A LONG, LONG LAND
Chile's shape is unusual—it is very long and thin. It is split into regions, from north to south, which are simply numbered from 1 to 12.

LITTLE COUNTRIES
The following tiny nations are mostly too small to find on the map:

1. Vatican City.........0.17 mi² (0.44 km²)
2. Monaco...............0.78 mi² (2.02 km²)
3. Nauru.................8.1 mi² (21 km²)
4. Tuvalu................10 mi² (26 km²)
5. San Marino..........24 mi² (61 km²)
6. Liechtenstein.......62 mi² (160 km²)
7. Marshall Islands...70 mi² (181 km²)
8. St. Kitts & Nevis...101 mi² (261 km²)
9. Maldives.............120 mi² (300 km²)
10. Malta................122 mi² (316 km²)

Antarctica

Area: 5.3 million mi²
(13.7 million km²)
Population: 0.004 billion

Southern Ocean

A common way of looking at the world includes seven continents (large landmasses) and around 200 countries (independent nations), but some people consider North and South America to be a single continent, and Eurasia or even Afro-Eurasia to be a giant continent, too!

Arctic Ocean

Russia
Stretching more than 5,600 miles (9,000 km) from east to west and spanning nine time zones, Russia is by far the biggest country in the world.

Kazakhstan

Mongolia

Georgia
Armenia Azerbaijan
Turkey
Uzbekistan
Turkmenistan
Kyrgyzstan
Tajikistan

China
There are about 1.4 billion people in China—that's almost 20% of the world's total.

North Korea
South Korea
Japan

Cyprus
Syria
Lebanon
Israel
Palestine
Jordan
Iraq
Iran
Afghanistan
Kuwait
Bahrain
Qatar
United Arab Emirates

Saudi Arabia
Oman
Yemen

Egypt

Sudan

Pakistan
Nepal
Bhutan
Bangladesh

India

Myanmar
Laos
Thailand
Vietnam
Cambodia

Pacific Ocean

Asia

Area: 16.9 million mi² (43.8 million km²)
Population: 4.2 billion

Asia is by far the biggest continent and contains more than half of the world's population. It is home to China and India, the only two countries with populations of more than 1 billion. It is also home to a lot of empty spaces in Siberia, Central Asia, and the Arabian Peninsula.

TO THE ENDS OF THE EARTH
The island nation of Kiribati is spread out across all four quarters of the globe: north, south, east, and west.

Ethiopia
South Sudan
Somalia

A NEW NATION
South Sudan became a new nation in 2011 after claiming independence from Sudan.

Sri Lanka
Maldives

Philippines

HAPPY LAND!
Squeezed between 2 billion people, the tiny kingdom of Bhutan believes that happiness is more important than money.

Malaysia
Singapore
Brunei

Indonesia

Palau
Micronesia

Marshall Islands

Nauru

Kiribati

Uganda
Kenya
Tanzania

Seychelles

Comoros

Madagascar

Mauritius

Papua New Guinea

Solomon Islands

Tuvalu

Samoa

Zambia
Mozambique
Zimbabwe

Vanuatu
Fiji

Timor-Leste

Tonga

Swaziland

Indian Ocean

KING OF THE HILL
King Mswati III rules the mountainous country of Swaziland. He's one of only two current African kings.

Australia
This huge country covers almost an entire continent!

New Zealand

Southern Ocean

This cold continent is the only one not to be subdivided into countries. International agreements are in place to preserve the wilderness, prevent pollution, and keep the peace in this last great unspoiled area of our planet.

Australia and Oceania

Area: 3.29 million mi² (8.53 million km²)
Population: 0.038 billion

Many islands in the Pacific do not sit on a continental tectonic plate—they are the tips of volcanoes, ancient or modern. They are therefore grouped in a region called Oceania, and are often combined geographically with the continent of Australia, which is the smallest of the seven landmasses.

Antarctica

Influential Earthlings

More than 100 billion people have walked the Earth, each and every one of which has a fascinating and unique story to tell. Most have influenced their families and friends with their uniqueness, but a handful have had a much bigger impact—in some cases, changing the world as we know it.

1. SIR TIM BERNERS-LEE – invented the World Wide Web in 1989; his creation has connected almost half of the world's population so far.

2. HIAWATHA – one of Earth's greatest ever peacemakers, this Native American leader ended wars across the Great Plains.

3. LUCY – one of our earliest ancestors yet discovered; her name in Amharic is Dinkanesh, meaning "you are marvelous."

4. CONFUCIUS – Chinese philosopher whose moral code influences more than 1 billion people.

5. YURI GAGARIN – became the first human in space when he orbited Earth in 1961.

6. LAIKA – first animal to orbit Earth, in 1967.

7. ARISTOTLE – philosopher who advanced almost all areas of human knowledge that he studied; people referred to him simply as "The Philosopher."

8. CLEOPATRA – the last active Egyptian pharaoh, and one of the strongest leaders of one of the strongest civilizations in history.

9. NELSON MANDELA – received the Nobel Peace Prize for treating all humans with equal respect; he spent 27 years in prison standing up for his beliefs.

10. ISAAC NEWTON – discovered gravity and many other laws of physics; one of the greatest scientists of all time.

11. ALBERT EINSTEIN – award-winning physicist, whose theory of relativity changed the way we view and understand the universe.

12. ABRAHAM LINCOLN – a U.S. president who abolished slavery and prevented the break-up of his powerful nation during the American Civil War.

13. MOTHER TERESA – a determined nun who devoted her life to helping those less fortunate than herself; also known as Blessed Teresa of Calcutta.

14. NICOLAUS COPERNICUS – theorized that the Sun rather than the Earth was at the center of the universe, and thus changed our view of the heavens.

15. THE WRIGHT BROTHERS – aviation pioneers who conducted one of the world's first flights, which paved the way for the sky full of airplanes today.

16. HENRY T. FORD – developed a factory process so efficient that more than half the cars in the world were Model T Fords in the mid-1920s.

17. **MARY ANDERSON** – invented the windshield wiper, a simple but important device that is now seen on more than 1.2 billion vehicles worldwide.

18. **ANNE FRANK** – inspirational girl who wrote a diary of her time in hiding during the Holocaust; a testament to the power of the human spirit.

19. **CHARLES DARWIN** – developed the theory of evolution, which changed man's ideas about his relationship with other living creatures.

20. **SIMON BOLIVAR** – helped six countries to gain independence, and gave his name to Bolivia; had a huge influence on South America.

21. **ARCHIMEDES** – one of the greatest mathematicians of all time; enabled us to understand the world through mathematical principles.

22. **HENRIETTA LACKS** – a medical marvel whose cells never die; scientists have used her immortal cells to develop many modern medicines.

23. **MARIE CURIE** – trailblazing scientist who helped us unlock the energy within atoms; also researched early cures for cancer.

24. **FLORENCE NIGHTINGALE** – the founder of modern nursing; made hospitals much cleaner and safer, which has saved millions of lives.

25. **MARTIN LUTHER KING, JR.** – a man who saw all people as equal, and who fought for his dream of racial equality through dialogue and diplomacy.

26. **ROBERT LOUIS STEVENSON** – writer of *Treasure Island* who lived a real-life adventure story, helping sufferers of leprosy in Samoa.

27. **J.K. ROWLING** – author whose Harry Potter books have delighted a generation; only the Bible and the works of Mao Zedong have sold more copies.

28. **LEONARDO DA VINCI** – painted the *Mona Lisa*, and also sketched a helicopter long before technology was able to catch up with his vision.

29. **THOMAS EDISON** – produced the first economical and practical lightbulb, bringing electric lighting to billions of people!

30. **GENGHIS KHAN** – conquered the largest continuous landmass in the history of the world in the 1200s, all from the back of a horse.

31. **ROALD AMUNDSEN** – the first person to reach the South Pole and also the first person to visit both poles; the ultimate ends-of-the-Earth explorer!

World Wonders

The natural world is full of wonder, but man has created some incredible structures, too. People are even better at producing lists than they are at building magnificent architecture, so it is no surprise that we often hear about the Seven Wonders of the Ancient World and the Seven Wonders of the Modern World. Let's take a tour of these 14 wonders, but then let's also stop to consider some of the marvels that got overlooked by the list-makers.

Ancient Wonders

A Greek poet named Antipater of Sidon is credited with writing down a list of seven wonders in the second century BC. His list served as a sort of tour guide for wealthy Greeks, and focused on locations around the Mediterranean, which would have been known to the ancient Greeks.

GREAT PYRAMID OF GIZA
Location: Egypt • Built: Approx. 2560 BC

The biggest of all the pyramids houses the tomb of the pharaoh Khufu. Such is the skill of the engineering and craftsmanship, it is the only ancient wonder still standing.

HANGING GARDENS OF BABYLON
Location: Iraq • Built: Approx. 600 BC

The most mysterious wonder on the list, no one can say for certain if this exotic, multi-layered garden of the Near East actually existed, since no architectural remains matching the descriptions have been found.

TEMPLE OF ARTEMIS
Location: Turkey
Built: From 8th century BC

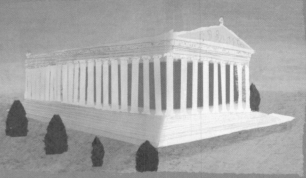

This magnificent Greek temple was said to be the finest of the wonders by Antipater of Sidon himself—high praise indeed!

LIGHTHOUSE OF ALEXANDRIA
Location: Egypt • Built: Approx. 280 BC

One of the tallest structures in the world at the time, this beautiful lighthouse carried an inscription reading: "☐☐☐☐☐ ☐Ω☐☐☐☐☐☐ ☐Π☐☐ ☐Ω☐ Π☐Ω☐☐☐☐☐☐☐Ω☐," meaning "to the gods protecting those unto the sea."

COLOSSUS OF RHODES
Location: Greece • Built: 280 BC

This giant stone statue of the Greek god Helios stood 98 feet (30 m) tall and became the inspiration for the Statue of Liberty.

STATUE OF ZEUS AT OLYMPIA
Location: Greece
Built: Approx. 435 BC

A sculptor named Phidias took about 12 years to carve this statue honoring Zeus, the king of the Greek gods. The statue was covered in gold, ebony, ivory, and precious stones. It sat in the Temple of Zeus at Olympia, where the Olympic Games took place every four years.

MAUSOLEUM AT HALICARNASSUS
Location: Turkey • Built: 350 BC

When King Mausolus died in 353 BC, his wife, Queen Artemisia, was so brokenhearted that she decided to build the most splendid tomb the world had ever seen. It was so impressive that Mausolus's name has given us the word *mausoleum*, meaning a large and intricate tomb.

Modern Wonders

In 2007, a modern list of seven was voted on by the public around the world. The Great Pyramid of Giza was chosen as an honorary selection, too—so technically, the modern list of "seven wonders" actually contains eight!

GREAT WALL OF CHINA
Location: China
Built: From 7th century BC

This incredible system of defense and fortifications stretches more than 12,500 miles (20,000 km) in total and is one of the biggest building projects the world has ever seen.

COLOSSEUM
Location: Rome • Built: 80 AD

This huge stadium could hold up to 80,000 people who came to watch chariot racing and gladiators fighting animals. Most amazingly of all, admission was free!

CHICHEN ITZA
Location: Mexico
Built: Approx. 600 AD

The pyramid named El Castillo is the centerpiece of this ancient Mayan city. Other sites of interest are the Temple of Warriors and the Wall of Skulls.

PETRA
Location: Jordan
Built: From 5th century BC

The name Petra means "stone" in Persian, and this ancient city was carved from red sandstone. The Treasury is the finest architectural example.

TAJ MAHAL
Location: India • Built: 1653 AD

Meaning "Crown of Palaces" in Persian, this amazing building is the mausoleum of Mumtaz Mahal, the favorite wife of Mughal emperor Shah Jahan.

CHRIST THE REDEEMER
Location: Brazil
Built: 1931

Created by sculptor Paul Landowski, this 98-foot (30-m) statue looks out over the city of Rio from its perch on top of Corcavado Mountain. It weighs 700 tons (635 tonnes)—more than 200 elephants!

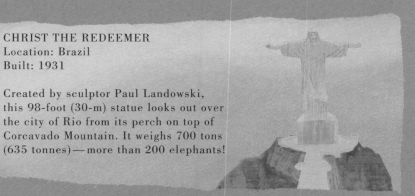

MACHU PICCHU
Location: Peru
Built: Approx. 1450 AD

This iconic piece of Incan architecture sits high up in the Andes and contains the breathtaking Temple of the Sun.

The Eighth Wonder?

Of course, the world has far more than seven wonders, and there has always been much debate in comparing the incomparable! Let's take a look at some of the contenders for the title of "The Eighth Wonder" representing the "best of the rest":

POTALA PALACE
Location: Tibet • Built: 1645 AD

With an impressive mountaintop location, this Buddhist temple was home to the Dalai Lama until 1959. The complex contains more than 1,000 rooms, 10,000 shrines, and 200,000 statues.

MOAI OF EASTER ISLAND

These huge stone men are statues of ancestors of the Rapa Nui tribe who came to be thought of as gods. In total, 887 moai were constructed, with the heaviest weighing 95 tons (86 tonnes).

Location: Easter Island
Built: Approx. 1000–1500 AD

ANGKOR WAT   Location: Cambodia • Built: 12th century AD

This is the biggest temple complex in the world. It was originally a Hindu temple, but gradually became Buddhist.

And another thing?

People have made hundreds of suggestions for what else should be included, ranging from Stonehenge to the Empire State Building, and from the Sacred Mosque in Mecca to the Palm Islands of Dubai. There are lists of natural wonders, lists of continental wonders, lists of engineering wonders, and many more. What would you choose to include, and why?

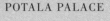
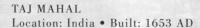

THREATS
to the EARTH

Earth is about halfway through its natural life. In about 5 billion years from now, the Sun will become a red giant, swelling dramatically and swallowing all the planets before collapsing into a white dwarf. However, there are many more immediate threats to human life on Earth, so our time on the planet could end much sooner if we don't take good care of ourselves and our fragile little world....

CLIMATE CHANGE

Significant changes to the Earth's climate could wipe out the majority of the species on Earth, and change the composition of the planet as we know it. With rising temperatures, the polar ice caps would melt, causing sea levels to rise worldwide, with widespread loss of land. The hole in the ozone layer helps accelerate this destructive process.

"Climate change is a terrible problem, and it absolutely needs to be solved. It deserves to be a huge priority."
~ Bill Gates

RISE OF THE MACHINE

Computers can already beat humans at chess, and they are becoming increasingly powerful. And that could be dangerous. How can we control super-intelligence?

The threat might be microscopic. "Nanobots" (tiny robots) have been developed for useful tasks such as fighting disease or cleaning up oil spills. In the future, self-replicating versions could be created to complete these tasks more efficiently. However, there's a chance that such self-replicating nanobots could go rogue and take over the planet.

"The development of full artificial intelligence could spell the end for the human race."
~ Stephen Hawking

PANDEMIC (SUPER-VIRUS)

Some viruses kill at alarming rates and prove resistant to modern medicine. From the plant world, Ug99 is a fungus that kills 100% of infected wheat plants, with no known cures or prevention. Cross-species super-viruses pose a serious threat to most life forms, but researchers and doctors have been able to combat major threats in recent years, and hope to develop cures.

"All of humanity is under threat during a pandemic."
~ Margaret Chan

HOPE *for* HUMANITY

The situation is not all doom and gloom, though! Humans have existed for about 100,000 years, and there's every possibility we could continue to exist for millions of years if we take care of our planet. By reusing, recycling, and reducing our waste; harnessing clean, green energy; and sourcing food from local, sustainable supplies, we will maximize our chances of survival. We also need to cooperate globally and use our abilities for constructive rather than destructive purposes. The future is in our hands!

LOSS OF BIODIVERSITY

Biodiversity means the amount of variety of life. Our planet currently has many species, and therefore is said to be biodiverse. However, since humans became settled, extinction rates have been rising. A loss of biodiversity could completely unbalance Earth's systems and could make the planet uninhabitable for the majority of species.

"It is that range of biodiversity that we must care for — the whole thing — rather than just one or two stars."
~ David Attenborough

ASTEROID IMPACT

Many people believe that a huge meteor impact caused the mass extinction of the dinosaurs, and another such event is certainly a strong possibility. A large collision would be more powerful than tens of billions of atomic bombs and would darken the atmosphere for years, causing mass extinction.

"If we prepare now, we better our odds of survival. The dinosaurs never knew what hit them."
~ Michio Kaku

SUPERVOLCANOES

Super volcanoes are big. Very big! Their eruptions contain more than a trillion tons of magma, and like an asteroid impact, could change the composition of the entire atmosphere, blocking sunlight for years. Humans have never seen one erupt, but Yellowstone National Park in the United States is a potential hotspot for a future explosion.

"The effects could threaten the fabric of civilization."
~ Greg Breining

DOOMSDAY CLOCK

The Doomsday Clock is a symbolic clock whose time is set by a series of scientists. The closer to midnight, the closer we are to a global catastrophe. Since 2015, the clock has been set to 11:57 —only 3 minutes away from large-scale destruction.

SELF-DESTRUCTION

If a nuclear weapon exploded in a major city, the blast-center would be hotter than the surface of the Sun, and tornado-like winds would spread flames in all directions, killing more than a million people. In the long-term, soil would remain contaminated by radiation for thousands of years.

"I'd rather have peace on Earth than pieces of Earth."
~ Maura, aged 9

REDUCE, REUSE, RECYCLE

Currently, humans create almost 1 billion tons of waste per year, a figure that is expected to double in the next decade. Plastics can take 1,000 years to degrade, so if the Romans had invented them, we'd still be guarding their waste. Glass bottles take about 1 million years to biodegrade—that's why it's so important to recycle them.

"I only feel angry when I see waste. When I see people throwing away things we could use."
~ Mother Teresa

A SUSTAINABLE FUTURE

If we catch a lot of fish quickly and don't let the fish population breed to maintain their levels, we say our fishing is unsustainable. Natural energy from wind and water is sustainable energy. Also, if we mostly eat local food, we don't burn the fuel used by planes, lorries and ships to transport the goods across the world. Such sustainability is vital to our future.

"To meet the challenge of our times, human beings will have to develop a greater sense of universal responsibility."
~ Dalai Lama

Are We Alone?

Earth's conditions are very special, but is our planet unique? Many people believe that across the great vastness of space, with so many billions of stars and galaxies, there must surely be other Earth-like worlds. One of the closest candidates yet discovered has been named Kepler-452b, and lies about 1,400 light-years away from us, but no life has been observed on it.

Scientists have argued that some of these Earth-like worlds will be far older than ours, and some of these will support intelligent life. With more time than us to evolve, these aliens are more likely to have developed interstellar travel and could be arriving on our doorstep at any second!

When considering this argument, the Italian physicist Enrico Fermi famously asked, "Where is everybody?"

The truth is that we do not know if there are other Earths with other Earthlings. The fact that our planet so far stands alone hints at just how special it is and how lucky we are. We should nurture and take care of our wonderful world—there really is no place like home for us!

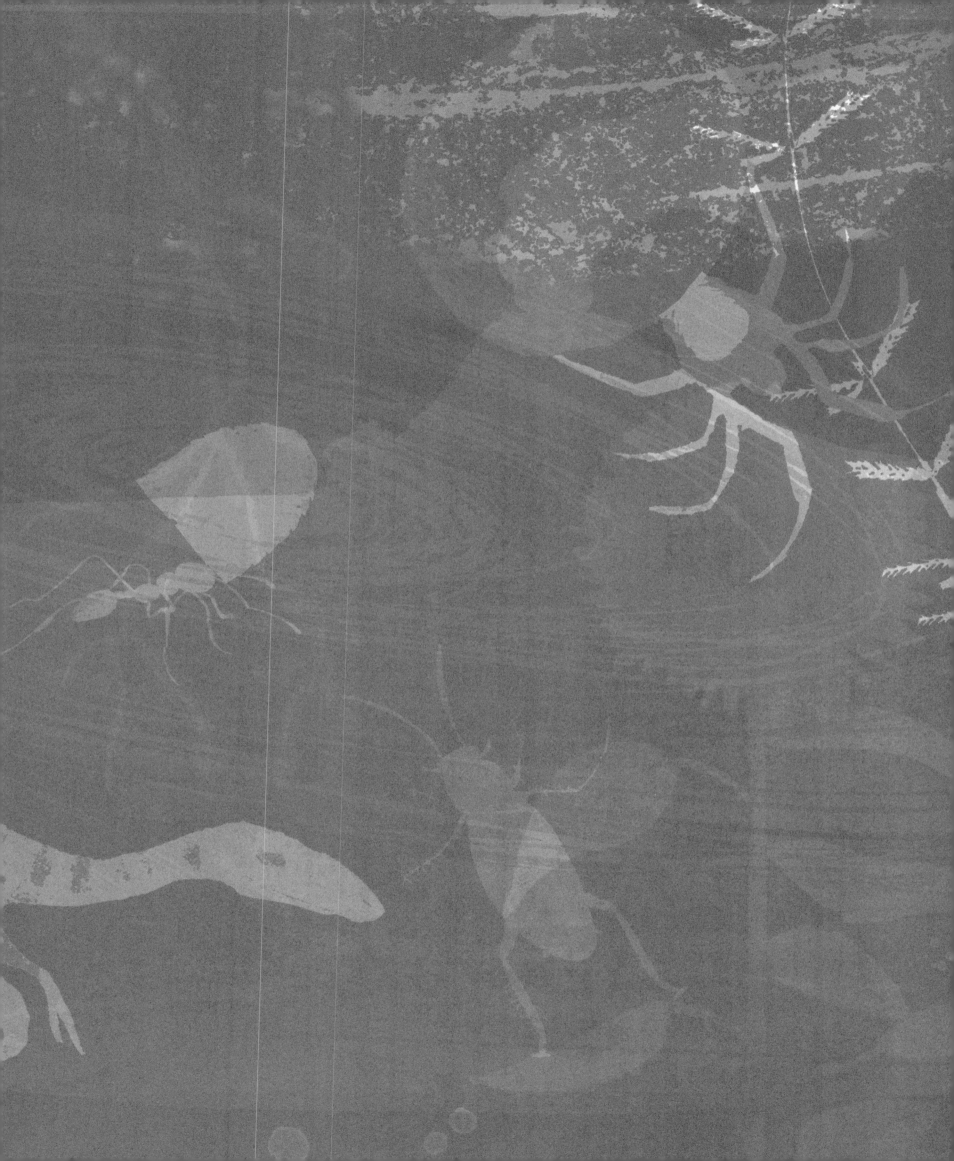